공무원 영어의 시작과 끝
이동기 영어

신경향

실전
어휘 &
생활영어
200제

기술을 익히는 데에는 '이론'과 '연습'이라는 두 가지 요소가 반드시 함께 있어야 합니다. 이론만 철저하게 익혔다고 해서 그 기술을 얻은 것도 아니고, 이론을 익히지 않고서는 연습은 아예 불가능합니다. 이렇게 이론을 익히고 꾸준한 연습을 하면 오랜 시간을 들이지 않고도 어렵지 않게 그 기술을 사용할 수 있는데 이를 '직관'적 기술의 사용이라고 할 수 있습니다.

시험의 기술도 예외는 아닙니다.

공무원 영어 시험에서 필요로 되는 이론을 정리하는 일이 우선시 되며, 이론을 실제 시험 문제에 적용할 수 있도록 충분한 연습을 하는 것이 뒤따라야 합니다. 그러면 비로소 실전 시험에서 직관적으로 정답을 선택할 수 있습니다. 즉, 빠르고 정확하게 정답을 고를 수 있다는 말입니다.

이 교재 <실전 어휘&생활영어 200제>는 시험에서 자주 출제되는 어휘, 표현, 생활영어 표현들을 정리하고, 직관적으로 문제를 풀 수 있을 만큼 충분한 연습을 할 수 있도록 기획되었습니다.

인사혁신처에서 발표한 출제 기조 전환에 따라 2025년 시험부터 공무원 영어 시험의 출제 유형이 달라집니다. 어휘 문제의 경우 그동안 밑줄 유의어 문제, 빈칸 완성 문제의 두 가지 유형이 출제되었고 단어뿐만 아니라 동사구나 관용 표현들도 출제되었다면 2025년 시험부터 밑줄 유의어 문제가 출제되지 않고 빈칸 완성 문제만 출제됩니다. 또한 지나치게 어려운 동사구나 관용 표현들도 출제되지 않을 것으로 예상됩니다. 인사혁신처는 이미 두 차례 예시문제를 공개하여 출제 기조의 전환을 분명히 밝혔습니다. 따라서 수험생들은 어휘의 암기만 되어 있다면 문장 전체를 읽어볼 필요 없이 밑줄 어휘만 보고 빠르게 문제를 해결하던 기존의 문제풀이법과는 전혀 다른 문제풀이법이 필요합니다. 이제는 어휘 암기뿐 아니라 문장에서 빈칸을 완성할만한 단서를 찾고 논리적인 추론을 통해 빈칸에 가장 적합한 어휘를 선택하는 문제풀이법에 대한 학습과 연습이 필요합니다. 또한 기존 출제되었던 어휘와는 범위가 다른 어휘가 출제될 것으로 예상되기에 출제 가능한 어휘의 범위를 파악해서 학습하는 선택과 집중이 무엇보다 중요합니다.

이동기 영어교육연구소는 인사혁신처의 출제 기조 전환에 대한 공지문과 두 차례 예시문제의 분석뿐 아니라 이를 기반으로 유사성이 보이는 공무원 기출문제, 토익문제, 수능문제 등 다양한 시험들을 모두 분석하여 출제 가능한 유형과 어휘들을 정리하여 공무원 영어 기본서인 [이동기 영어 신경향 올인원]에 수록했습니다. 또한 이런 유형분석을 기반으로 인사혁신처에서 발표한 예시문제와 가장 유사한 문제들, 그리고 출제 가능한 문제들을 직접 출제하고 여러 차례 감수를 거쳐 이번 [실전 어휘&생활영어 200제]를 출간하게 되었습니다.

[실전 어휘&생활영어 200제] 이 한 권으로 새롭게 바뀌는 시험에 완벽히 대비할 수 있다고 자신합니다.

이 교재가 수험생들이 원하는 합격 점수 확보로 가는 과정에 있어 최종 연습서가 되기 바라며 본서로 문제풀이 능력을 기른 모든 수험생들이 시험에서 '합격'이라는 결과를 얻을 수 있도록 이 교재에 많은 정성과 혼을 불어넣었습니다.

좋은 문제를 선별하고, 친절하고 꼼꼼한 해설을 작성할 수 있도록 도와준 이동기 영어교육연구소의 연구원들에게 감사의 말을 전하고 싶습니다.

마지막으로, 진정으로 합격을 갈구하며 하루도 빠짐없이 어두운 새벽부터 힘차게 하루를 시작하는 모든 제자들에게 격려와 응원의 말을 전하고 싶습니다.

여러분의 합격을 기원합니다.

2024년 9월 연구실에서

이동기 드림

교재 활용법

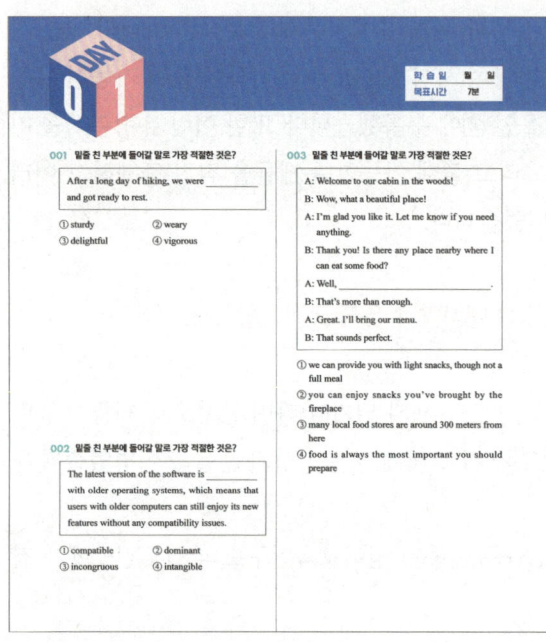

STEP 1

하루 정해진 분량(하루 10개)의 문제를 시간을 재며 먼저 풀어봅니다. 권장하는 문제 개수와 시간은 다음과 같습니다.

권장 문제 개수	10개/1일
문제당 시간	30~50초

STEP 2

각 문제의 오른쪽에 해당하는 페이지에 수록된 정답과 해설 부분을 읽고 근거를 파악해가며 꼼꼼히 학습합니다.

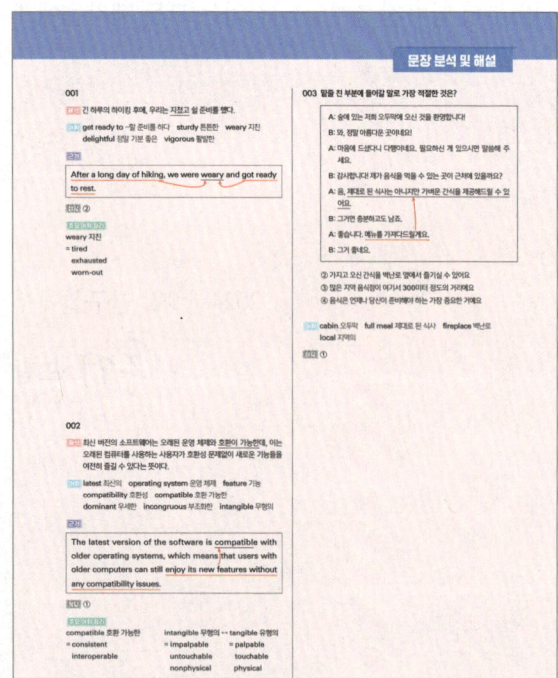

STEP 3

200문제를 모두 푼 후 전체 200문제 중 틀린 문제나 중요하다고 표시해 둔 문제들만 다시 꼼꼼하게 분석합니다. 내가 고른 선택지가 왜 오답인지, 그리고 정답인 선택지에 대한 근거를 정확히 찾는 등 꼼꼼한 분석이 필요합니다.

구성과 특징

1. 엄선된 최빈출 어휘와 생활영어 표현
- 인사혁신처 신경향 출제 기조를 반영한 신경향 문제 수록
- 최근 10년간의 기출문제를 중심으로 선별된 최빈출 어휘 문제 수록
- 난이도 중~상의 실전문제 수록
- 국가직, 통합 지방직, 교행 등 올해 시험에서 적중으로 입증된 선별된 문제 수록

2. 자습에 최적화된 해설과 해석
- 전 문항 꼼꼼한 해설과 해석
- 상세한 유의어와 유사 표현 정리
- 각 문제별 정답에 대한 명확한 근거 표시

3. 매일 학습을 고려한 문제 구성
- 문제 구성에 있어 어휘, 표현, 생활영어 문제를 번갈아 가며 출제
- 하루 10개의 문제 풀이 권장

4. 온라인을 통한 학습 지원
- 동영상 강의(gong.conects.com)를 통해 시간은 적게 들고 문제풀이 방법은 정확히 학습하는 시간 효율적인 학습
- 카페(daum '이동기 공무원 영어')를 통한 질문과 답변, 상담

CONTENTS
차례

DAY 01	10		**DAY 11**	90
DAY 02	18		**DAY 12**	98
DAY 03	26		**DAY 13**	106
DAY 04	34		**DAY 14**	114
DAY 05	42		**DAY 15**	122
DAY 06	50		**DAY 16**	130
DAY 07	58		**DAY 17**	138
DAY 08	66		**DAY 18**	146
DAY 09	74		**DAY 19**	154
DAY 10	82		**DAY 20**	162

20일 완성 학습 플랜
하루 10문제를 매일 풀어 20일을 완성합니다.

1일 완료	2일 완료	3일 완료	4일 완료
DAY 01	DAY 02	DAY 03	DAY 04

5일 완료	6일 완료	7일 완료	8일 완료
DAY 05	DAY 06	DAY 07	DAY 08

9일 완료	10일 완료	11일 완료	12일 완료
DAY 09	DAY 10	DAY 11	DAY 12

13일 완료	14일 완료	15일 완료	16일 완료
DAY 13	DAY 14	DAY 15	DAY 16

17일 완료	18일 완료	19일 완료	20일 완료
DAY 17	DAY 18	DAY 19	DAY 20

선별된
200문제로
깔끔하고 빈틈없이
정리하는
어휘·생활영어

학습일　월　일
목표시간　7분

001 밑줄 친 부분에 들어갈 말로 가장 적절한 것은?

> After a long day of hiking, we were _____ and got ready to rest.

① sturdy　② weary
③ delightful　④ vigorous

002 밑줄 친 부분에 들어갈 말로 가장 적절한 것은?

> The latest version of the software is _____ with older operating systems, which means that users with older computers can still enjoy its new features without any compatibility issues.

① compatible　② dominant
③ incongruous　④ intangible

003 밑줄 친 부분에 들어갈 말로 가장 적절한 것은?

> A: Welcome to our cabin in the woods!
> B: Wow, what a beautiful place!
> A: I'm glad you like it. Let me know if you need anything.
> B: Thank you! Is there any place nearby where I can eat some food?
> A: Well, _____.
> B: That's more than enough.
> A: Great. I'll bring our menu.
> B: That sounds perfect.

① we can provide you with light snacks, though not a full meal
② you can enjoy snacks you've brought by the fireplace
③ many local food stores are around 300 meters from here
④ food is always the most important you should prepare

문장 분석 및 해설

001

해석 긴 하루의 하이킹 후에, 우리는 지쳤고 쉴 준비를 했다.

어휘 get ready to ~할 준비를 하다　sturdy 튼튼한　weary 지친
delightful 정말 기분 좋은　vigorous 활발한

근거

> After a long day of hiking, we were weary and got ready to rest.

정답 ②

주요 어휘 정리

weary 지친
= tired
　exhausted
　worn-out

sturdy 튼튼한
= strong
　robust

002

해석 최신 버전의 소프트웨어는 오래된 운영 체제와 호환이 가능한데, 이는 오래된 컴퓨터를 사용하는 사용자가 호환성 문제없이 새로운 기능들을 여전히 즐길 수 있다는 뜻이다.

어휘 latest 최신의　operating system 운영 체제　feature 기능
compatibility 호환성　compatible 호환 가능한
dominant 우세한　incongruous 부조화한　intangible 무형의

근거

> The latest version of the software is compatible with older operating systems, which means that users with older computers can still enjoy its new features without any compatibility issues.

정답 ①

주요 어휘 정리

compatible 호환 가능한
= consistent
　harmonious
　congruous
　congruent

intangible 무형의 ↔ tangible 유형의
= impalpable　　= palpable
　untouchable　　touchable
　nonphysical　　physical
　abstract　　　concrete

003 밑줄 친 부분에 들어갈 말로 가장 적절한 것은?

A: 숲에 있는 저희 오두막에 오신 것을 환영합니다!

B: 와, 정말 아름다운 곳이네요!

A: 마음에 드셨다니 다행이네요. 필요하신 게 있으시면 말씀해 주세요.

B: 감사합니다! 제가 음식을 먹을 수 있는 곳이 근처에 있을까요?

A: 음, 제대로 된 식사는 아니지만 가벼운 간식을 제공해드릴 수 있어요.

B: 그거면 충분하고도 남죠.

A: 좋습니다. 메뉴를 가져다드릴게요.

B: 그거 좋네요.

② 가지고 오신 간식을 벽난로 옆에서 즐기실 수 있어요
③ 많은 지역 음식점이 여기서 300미터 정도의 거리에요
④ 음식은 언제나 당신이 준비해야 하는 가장 중요한 거예요

어휘 cabin 오두막　full meal 제대로 된 식사　fireplace 벽난로
local 지역의

정답 ①

DAY 01　11

학습일 월 일
목표시간 7분

004 밑줄 친 부분에 들어갈 말로 가장 적절한 것은?

> With determination and perseverance, he was able to _____ his fear of public speaking.

① defend ② shield
③ infringe ④ conquer

005 밑줄 친 부분에 들어갈 말로 가장 적절한 것은?

> To resolve the conflict between the two departments, the manager _____ a discussion to find a mutually acceptable solution.

① ignored ② escalated
③ mediated ④ postponed

006 밑줄 친 부분에 들어갈 말로 가장 적절한 것은?

> A: Your presentation was impressive. You really nailed it.
> B: I appreciate your kind words.
> A: That really was great, especially that last part.
> B: It's nice to hear that my hard work paid off.
> A: May I add a point or two, _____.
> B: Good insight! I'll keep that in mind for future reference.

① I didn't have time to put much effort into that
② it could've been better with more visual materials
③ I have a few suggestions you might want to consider
④ it was done without reference to you or your team

004

해석 그는 결단력과 끈기로 대중 연설에 대한 두려움을 극복할 수 있었다.

어휘 determination 결단력 perseverance 끈기 fear 두려움
public speaking 대중 연설 defend 방어하다 shield 보호하다
infringe 침해하다 conquer 극복하다

근거

> With determination and perseverance, he was able to conquer his fear of public speaking.

정답 ④

주요 어휘 정리

conquer 극복하다	infringe 침해하다, 위반하다
= overcome	= encroach, trespass 침해하다
master	break, breach 위반하다
defeat	violate
surmount	

005

해석 두 부서 간의 갈등을 해결하기 위해, 매니저는 서로 수용할 수 있는 해결책을 찾기 위한 논의를 중재했다.

어휘 resolve 해결하다 conflict 갈등 department 부서
discussion 논의 mutually 서로 acceptable 수용할 수 있는
ignore 무시하다 escalate 확대시키다 mediate 중재하다
postpone 연기하다

근거

> To resolve the conflict between the two departments, the manager mediated a discussion to find a mutually acceptable solution.

정답 ③

주요 어휘 정리

mediate 중재하다	escalate 확대시키다
= arbitrate	= grow
conciliate	develop
	increase

006 밑줄 친 부분에 들어갈 말로 가장 적절한 것은?

> A: 발표가 인상적이었어요. 정말 잘했어요.
> B: 좋은 말씀 해주셔서 감사합니다.
> A: 정말로 좋았거든요, 특히 그 마지막 부분이요.
> B: 열심히 노력한 보람이 있다는 말을 들으니 좋네요.
> A: 한두 마디만 덧붙이자면, 시각적인 자료가 더 많았으면 더 좋았을 것 같아요.
> B: 통찰력이 좋으시네요! 다음에 참고할 수 있게 그걸 명심할게요.

① 그 일에 많은 노력을 쏟아부을 시간이 없었어요
③ 당신이 고려할 만한 몇 가지 제안이 있어요
④ 그 일은 당신이나 당신 팀과 관계없이 실행되었어요

어휘 seriously 진심으로 presentation 발표 impressive 인상적인
You nailed it. 잘했어요. appreciate 감사하다
pay off 보람이 있다 insight 통찰력 keep in mind ~을 명심하다
for future reference 다음에 참고할 수 있게 effort 노력
visual 시각의 materials 자료 suggestion 제안
without reference to ~와 관계없이

정답 ②

007 밑줄 친 부분에 들어갈 말로 가장 적절한 것은?

Lily Harris
How did you like the independent film I recommended?
10:42

Brian Nelson
I really enjoyed it! The story was so refreshing. I've never seen anything like it before.
10:43

Lily Harris
The director always tries new and creative things.
10:44

Brian Nelson
He created remarkable scenes using impressive color and sound effects.
10:45

Lily Harris
You are right. And the director is famous for creating unique characters.
10:46

Brian Nelson
Oh, _____?
10:47

Lily Harris
Then, I'll give you a list of his best films.
10:48

① would you like go to see blockbusters together
② can you recommend his other movies to watch
③ is that why you prefer watching popular movies
④ do you think his work is a total flop of a movie

008 밑줄 친 부분에 들어갈 말로 가장 적절한 것은?

A: Did you catch that documentary everyone's talking about?
B: Yeah, it was eye-opening.
A: What struck you the most about the documentary?
B: The visuals of melting ice caps were powerful.
A: Right, the impact of climate change is a critical issue.
B: _____.
A: There are plenty of people just like you. So, it's important to promote global warming to the public.

① I hadn't realized how important it was until I saw that
② I usually watch documentaries whenever I have time
③ After watching that, a happy thought struck me
④ I always put weight on promoting environmental issues

007 밑줄 친 부분에 들어갈 말로 가장 적절한 것은?

① 블록버스터 영화를 같이 보러 갈래요
③ 그런 이유로 인기 영화 보는 걸 좋아하시나요
④ 그의 작품이 완전히 망한 영화라고 생각하세요

어휘 independent 독립의   film 영화   recommend 추천하다
refreshing 신선한   director 감독   creative 창의적인
remarkable 주목할 만한   scene 장면   impressive 인상적인
sound effect 음향 효과   prefer 선호하다   total flop 망작

정답 ②

008 밑줄 친 부분에 들어갈 말로 가장 적절한 것은?

> A: 모두가 이야기하는 그 다큐멘터리 봤어?
> B: 응, 놀라웠어.
> A: 다큐멘터리에서 무엇이 가장 강한 인상을 주었어?
> B: 녹아내리는 만년설의 영상이 강렬했어.
> A: 그래, 기후변화의 영향은 아주 중요한 문제야.
> B: 그 다큐멘터리를 보기 전까지는 그게 얼마나 중요한지 몰랐어.
> A: 너 같은 사람들이 많아. 그래서, 지구 온난화를 대중에게 널리 알리는 게 중요한 거야.

② 나는 시간이 날 때마다 대개 다큐멘터리를 봐
③ 그걸 시청한 뒤에, 행복한 생각이 떠올랐어
④ 나는 환경 문제를 널리 알리는 것을 항상 중요하게 여겨

어휘 catch (방송 등을) 보다   eye-opening 놀랄 만한
strike 강한 인상을 주다, 떠오르다   ice cap 만년설   impact 영향
plenty of 많은   promote 널리 알리다
put weight on ~을 중요하게 여기다   environmental 환경의

정답 ①

009 밑줄 친 부분에 들어갈 말로 가장 적절한 것은?

Mark Allen
Jenny, I'm afraid I cannot make it to our book club today. So, will you and David meet without me?
10:42

Jenny Campbell
Well... I have to miss it, too. I have an upset stomach.
10:43

Mark Allen
That means only David will be there. It seems we cannot meet today. What should we do?
10:44

Jenny Campbell
_____
_____
10:45

① Why don't you put off visiting the doctor?
② Let's ask David if we can reschedule.
③ How about inviting David to our club?
④ We should find a place for today's meeting.

010 밑줄 친 부분에 들어갈 말로 가장 적절한 것은?

China's newest entrants to the workforce have been struggling with a difficult job market for years, but since the pandemic the situation has even _____ dramatically.

① deteriorated   ② acclaimed
③ rebelled   ④ replicated

009 밑줄 친 부분에 들어갈 말로 가장 적절한 것은?

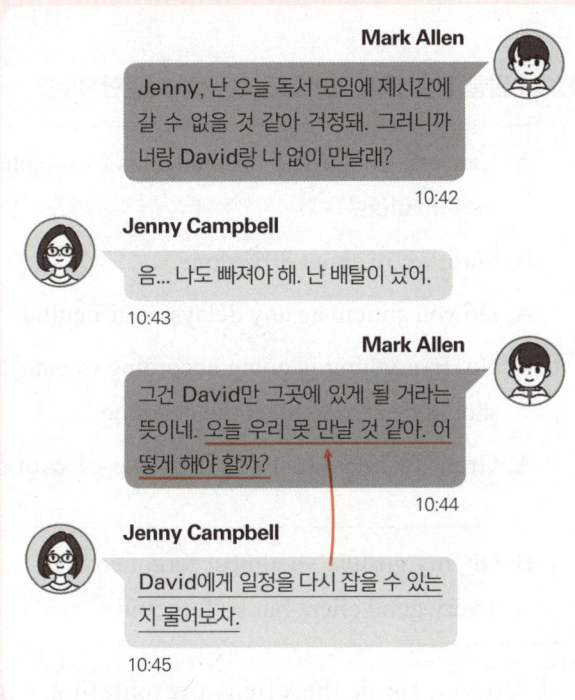

① 병원 방문을 미루는 게 어때?
③ David를 우리 모임에 초대하는 거 어때?
④ 오늘 모임을 위한 장소를 찾아야 해.

어휘 afraid 걱정되는 make it 제시간에 가다 miss 빠지다
upset stomach 배탈 put off 미루다
reschedule 일정을 다시 잡다 invite 초대하다

정답 ②

010

해석 중국의 노동인구 신규 진입자들은 어려운 고용 시장으로 수년 동안 허덕이고 있지만, 팬데믹 이후 상황은 심지어 급격히 악화되었다.

어휘 entrant 진입자   workforce 노동인구   dramatically 급격히
deteriorate 악화되다   acclaim 칭송하다   rebel 저항하다
replicate 복제하다

근거

China's newest entrants to the workforce have been struggling with a difficult job market for years, but since the pandemic the situation has even deteriorated dramatically.

정답 ①

주요 어휘 정리

deteriorate 악화되다, 나빠지다
= worsen
  degenerate

rebel 저항하다, 반대하다
= oppose
  resist
  defy
  disobey

DAY 01 17

011 밑줄 친 부분에 들어갈 말로 가장 적절한 것은?

> Most legal strategies assume that the _____ evidence is final; however, this doesn't account for new conclusive findings that may emerge during the trial.

① incessant
② subsequent
③ versatile
④ preliminary

012 밑줄 친 부분에 들어갈 말로 가장 적절한 것은?

> During the hot summer days, puddles of water quickly _____ under the scorching sun, leaving behind dry pavement.

① evolve
② evaporate
③ revolve
④ erode

013 밑줄 친 부분에 들어갈 말로 가장 적절한 것은?

> A: Can you update me on the status of the client presentation?
> B: Sure, we're about 80% done.
> A: Do you anticipate any delays or difficulties?
> B: No. Everything is going according to plan. We should be able to meet the deadline.
> A: Great to hear. Just for the sake of caution, _____
> B: Oh, my gosh! I've almost forgotten that. He is a very good client but so forgetful.

① Do you think the client presentation will be successful?
② you should check if the client remembers the date.
③ Do you know the final review is scheduled for today?
④ I have finalized the budget for the next client presentation.

011

해석 대부분의 법률 전략은 예비 증거가 최종적인 것으로 가정한다; 그러나, 이는 재판 과정에서 드러날 수 있는 새로운 결정적인 결과를 설명하지 못한다.

어휘 strategy 전략 assume 추정하다 evidence 증거
account for 설명하다 conclusive 결정적인 emerge 드러나다
incessant 끊임없는 subsequent 차후의 versatile 다재다능한
preliminary 예비의

근거

> Most legal strategies assume that the preliminary evidence is final; however, this doesn't account for new conclusive findings that may emerge during the trial.

정답 ④

주요 어휘 정리

preliminary 예비의
= introductory
  preparatory

versatile 다재다능한, 다용도의
= all-round
  all-purpose
  adaptable
  flexible

012

해석 무더운 여름날 동안 물웅덩이는 몹시 뜨거운 햇볕 아래에서 빠르게 증발하여 마른 노면을 남긴다.

어휘 puddle 물웅덩이 scorching 몹시 뜨거운
leave behind ~을 남기다 pavement 노면 evolve 진화하다
evaporate 증발하다 revolve 회전하다 erode 침식하다

근거

> During the hot summer days, puddles of water quickly evaporate under the scorching sun, leaving behind dry pavement.

정답 ②

주요 어휘 정리

evaporate 증발하다
= dry up

revolve 회전하다
= turn
  rotate
  whirl
  spin

013 밑줄 친 부분에 들어갈 말로 가장 적절한 것은?

> A: 고객 프레젠테이션 상황을 업데이트 해주시겠어요?
> B: 물론이죠, 약 80퍼센트 완료되었어요.
> A: 어떤 지연이나 어려움이 예상되나요?
> B: 아니오. 모든 것이 계획대로 진행되고 있어요. 마감 기한을 지킬 수 있을 거예요.
> A: 좋은 소식이네요. 단지 노파심에서 그러는데요, 고객이 날짜를 기억하는지 확인하는 게 좋겠어요.
> B: 오, 세상에! 하마터면 그걸 잊어버릴 뻔했어요. 그분은 아주 좋은 고객이지만 건망증이 심하거든요.

① 고객 프레젠테이션이 성공할 거라고 생각하나요?
③ 최종 검토가 오늘 예정된 걸 아시나요?
④ 다음 고객 프레젠테이션 예산을 확정했어요.

어휘 status 상황 anticipate 예상하다 delay 지연
meet the deadline 마감 기한을 지키다
for the sake of caution 노파심에서 forgetful 건망증이 있는
finalize 확정하다 budget 예산

정답 ②

014 밑줄 친 부분에 들어갈 말로 가장 적절한 것은?

> A: Do I need to bring anything to the party?
> B: No, you need a good mood and a smile. We've got everything covered. It's going to be a casual get-together with drinks and snacks.
> A: That sounds easy enough. When does the party start?
> B: At 7 PM. _____
> A: Got it, I'll be there around 7:30, then.
> B: Perfect! Looking forward to catching up with.

① We're keeping it relaxed, so no rush.
② You can show up on time, right?
③ We will save a spot for you.
④ Don't be tardy for the party as usual.

015 밑줄 친 부분에 들어갈 말로 가장 적절한 것은?

> Instead of _____ any important data, make sure you include all relevant information when preparing the report to influence the final decision.

① covering   ② grasping
③ involving   ④ omitting

016 밑줄 친 부분에 들어갈 말로 가장 적절한 것은?

> Despite numerous attempts to change his mind, he remained _____ and refused to listen to any alternative opinions.

① humble   ② obstinate
③ diligent   ④ intellectual

014 밑줄 친 부분에 들어갈 말로 가장 적절한 것은?

> A: 파티에 뭔가를 가져가야 하나요?
> B: 아니오, 좋은 기분과 미소만 있으면 돼요. 저희가 모든 걸 책임지니까요. 술과 간식이 있는 가벼운 모임이 될 거예요.
> A: 충분히 부담이 없겠네요. 파티가 언제 시작하나요?
> B: 오후 7시요. 편하게 하려고 하니까, 서두를 건 없어요.
> A: 알겠어요, 그러면, 7시 반쯤에 갈게요.
> B: 완벽하네요! 밀린 이야기를 나누길 기대할게요.

② 정시에 나타날 수 있죠, 그렇죠?
③ 당신 자리를 맡아둘게요.
④ 평소처럼 파티에 늦지 마세요.

어휘 cover 책임지다 casual 가벼운 get-together 모임 rush 서두름
look forward to ~을 기대하다
catch up with ~와 밀린 이야기를 하다 show up 나타나다
on time 정시에 tardy 늦은 as usual 평소처럼

정답 ①

015

해석 중요한 자료를 제외시키는 대신 최종 결정에 영향을 미치기 위해 보고서를 준비할 때 모든 관련 정보를 반드시 포함해야 한다.

어휘 make sure 반드시 ~하다 include 포함하다 relevant 연관된
influence 영향을 주다 cover 다루다 grasp 움켜잡다
involve 포함하다 omit 제외시키다

근거

> Instead of omitting any important data, make sure you include all relevant information when preparing the report to influence the final decision.

정답 ④

주요 어휘 정리
omit 누락시키다   include 포함시키다
= leave out   = contain
                             cover
                             incorporate

016

해석 그의 마음을 바꾸려는 수많은 시도에도 불구하고, 그는 여전히 고집이 셌고, 어떤 대안적인 의견도 듣기를 거부했다.

어휘 numerous 수많은 attempt 시도 refuse 거부하다
alternative 대안적인 humble 겸손한 obstinate 고집 센
diligent 부지런한 intellectual 지적인

근거

> Despite numerous attempts to change his mind, he remained obstinate and refused to listen to any alternative opinions.

정답 ②

주요 어휘 정리
obstinate 고집 센
= stubborn
  inflexible
  tenacious
  intractable
  persistent
  unadaptable
  headstrong

017 밑줄 친 부분에 들어갈 말로 가장 적절한 것은?

> A: Wow, your garden always looks so colorful and vibrant.
> B: Thanks. How about our garden this year?
> A: It's been a challenge with all the rain so far.
> B: That's a pity. _____?
> A: I'm trying out different herbs varieties, and planning to install an automated irrigation system.
> B: Sounds great. You seem fully geared up.

① Why don't you give up gardening at all
② What type of soil did you use for your plants
③ Haven't you built a glass green house
④ Have you come up with any solution

018 밑줄 친 부분에 들어갈 말로 가장 적절한 것은?

> A: Have you read any good books lately?
> B: Yeah, I just finished a gripping mystery novel. It kept me on edge until the end.
> A: Those are the best kind. _____?
> B: I didn't see the identity of the culprit coming at all. It was cleverly written.
> A: Sounds like a page-turner. I'll add it to my reading list.

① How many points would you give the book
② What did you think of the book's pacing
③ What was the plot twist that surprised you
④ How did the setting influence the story

017 밑줄 친 부분에 들어갈 말로 가장 적절한 것은?

> A: 와, 네 정원은 언제나 다채롭고 생기가 넘쳐 보여.
> B: 고마워. 네 정원은 올해 어때?
> A: 지금까지는 비가 많이 와서 힘들었어.
> B: 그것참 안됐구나. 어떤 해결책이라도 생각해냈어?
> A: 다양한 허브 품종을 시도해 보는 중이고, 자동 급수 시스템도 설치할 계획이야.
> B: 멋지다. 넌 준비가 완벽히 된 것 같아.

① 원예를 완전히 포기하는 게 어때
② 네 식물에 어떤 종류의 흙을 사용했어
③ 유리 온실을 설치하지 않았어

어휘 vibrant 생기가 넘치는   That's a pity. 그것참 안됐다.
variety 품종   install 설치하다   automated 자동의
irrigation 급수   gear up ~에게 준비를 갖추게 하다
come up with ~을 생각해내다

정답 ④

018 밑줄 친 부분에 들어갈 말로 가장 적절한 것은?

> A: 최근에 좋은 책 읽어본 것 있어?
> B: 응, 방금 눈을 떼지 못하게 하는 추리소설을 다 읽었어. 그 책은 마지막까지 내가 계속 마음 졸이게 만들었어.
> A: 그런 것들이 최고의 종류지. 너를 놀라게 한 뜻밖의 반전은 무엇이었어?
> B: 난 범인의 신원을 전혀 몰랐어. 그건 교묘하게 쓰여졌어.
> A: 흥미진진한 책인 것 같네. 내 독서 목록에 그걸 추가해야겠어.

① 그 책에 몇 점을 주고 싶어
② 책의 전개 속도는 어땠다고 생각해
④ 배경이 어떻게 그 책에 영향을 주었어

어휘 gripping 눈을 떼지 못하게 하는   mystery novel 추리소설
on edge 마음 졸이는   identity 신원   culprit 범인
I don't see ~ coming at all. ~을 전혀 모르다   cleverly 교묘하게
page-turner 흥미진진한 책   plot twist 뜻밖의 반전   setting 배경

정답 ③

019 밑줄 친 부분에 들어갈 말로 가장 적절한 것은?

Kelly Parker
Willy, what are you doing?
10:42

Willy Adams
Hi, Kelly! I'm making plans to run for president of the student council.
10:43

Kelly Parker
Really? I heard Angela is also going to run for the position.
10:44

Willy Adams
I didn't know she was interested.
10:45

Kelly Parker
Her friends want to make her student council president.
10:46

Willy Adams
Good for her! I hope my friends help me, too.
10:47

Kelly Parker
I want to assist you in any way I can. Is there anything I can do?
10:48

Willy Adams
You got first prize in the drawing contest, didn't you?
10:49

Kelly Parker
Yeah, but how can that help you?
10:50

Willy Adams
_____
_____.
10:51

① Let's invite other members to our club
② You can make election campaign posters for me
③ Don't worry, I'll vote against her in this election
④ Please check if she runs for student council president

020 밑줄 친 부분에 들어갈 말로 가장 적절한 것은?

The Ministry of Finance has asked all infrastructure-related ministries to evaluate delayed infrastructure projects and _____ solutions that can be implemented. The ministries are expected to prepare a status report by November.

① withdraw   ② propose
③ discard   ④ repeal

019 밑줄 친 부분에 들어갈 말로 가장 적절한 것은?

① 다른 회원들을 우리 동아리에 초대하자.
③ 걱정하지 마, 나는 이번 선거에서 그녀에게 반대하는 투표를 할 거야.
④ 그녀가 학생회장 선거에 출마하는지 확인해줘.

어휘 president 회장   student council 학생회   run for ~에 출마하다
invite 초대하다   election 선거   vote 투표하다
against ~에 반대하는

정답 ②

020

해석 재정부는 모든 기반시설 관련 부처에 지연된 기반시설 프로젝트를 평가해서 실행할 수 있는 해결책을 내놓으라고 요청했다. 그 부처들은 11월까지 현황 보고서를 준비할 것으로 기대된다.

어휘 Ministry of Finance 재정부   infrastructure 기반시설
evaluate 평가하다   implement 실행하다
status report 현황 보고서   withdraw 철회하다
propose 제시하다   discard 버리다   repeal 폐지하다

근거

> The Ministry of Finance has asked all infrastructure-related ministries to evaluate delayed infrastructure projects and propose solutions that can be implemented. The ministries are expected to prepare a status report by November.

정답 ②

주요 어휘 정리

propose 제시하다, 내놓다	withdraw 철회하다
= suggest	= retreat
come up with	repeal
bring up	pull out
put forth	abolish
set forth	

discard 버리다, 포기하다
= abandon
  forgo
  forsake
  relinquish
  renounce

021 밑줄 친 부분에 들어갈 말로 가장 적절한 것은?

> She decided to _____ voting on the controversial proposal to avoid influencing the outcome unfairly.

① scrutinize   ② quell
③ investigate   ④ relinquish

022 밑줄 친 부분에 들어갈 말로 가장 적절한 것은?

> The volcano had been _____ for centuries, but suddenly showed signs of activity with small tremors and minor eruptions.

① distant   ② nocturnal
③ active   ④ dormant

023 밑줄 친 부분에 들어갈 말로 가장 적절한 것은?

> A: I think we're going to have a great time as roommates.
> B: Are you a morning person or a night person?
> A: I'm very flexible with sleeping times. _____
> B: I should be fine too unless you blast the music while I'm sleeping.
> A: Great! By the way, did you eat lunch yet?
> B: No. Is there a cafeteria in the building?
> A: Yeah. I'll show you.

① I think I'm a morning person.
② How do you like the music?
③ They have a strict rule about noise level.
④ Besides, a little noise never bothers me.

문장 분석 및 해설

021

해석 그녀는 결과에 불공정하게 영향을 주는 것을 피하기 위해 그 논란이 많은 제안에 대한 투표를 포기하기로 결정했다.

어휘 vote 투표하다 controversial 논란이 많은 proposal 제안 avoid 피하다 outcome 결과 unfairly 부정하게 scrutinize 조사하다 quell 진압하다 investigate 조사하다 relinquish 포기하다

근거

> She decided to relinquish voting on the controversial proposal to avoid influencing the outcome unfairly.

정답 ④

주요 어휘 정리

relinquish 포기하다	investigate ~을 철저하게 조사하다	
= abandon	= inspect	look into
renounce	scrutinize	delve into
forsake	examine	probe into
forgo		go over
give up		pore over

022

해석 그 화산은 수 세기 동안 휴면 상태였으나 갑자기 작은 진동과 작은 분출로 활동 징후를 보였다.

어휘 volcano 화산 century 세기 sign 징후 tremor 진동 minor 작은 eruption 분출 distant 먼 nocturnal 야행성의 active 활동적인 dormant 휴면의

근거

> The volcano had been dormant for centuries, but suddenly showed signs of activity with small tremors and minor eruptions.

정답 ④

주요 어휘 정리

dormant 휴면의	distant 먼
= inactive	= far
inert	remote
static	
dormant	
stagnant	

023 밑줄 친 부분에 들어갈 말로 가장 적절한 것은?

A: 우리가 룸메이트로서 즐거운 시간을 보낼 수 있을 것 같네요.
B: 아침형 인간이세요, 저녁형 인간이세요?
A: 저는 잠자는 시간에 굉장히 유연해요. 게다가, 조금 시끄러운 것은 절대 신경 쓰지 않아요.
B: 제가 자는 동안 당신이 음악을 크게 틀어대지만 않는다면, 저도 괜찮아요.
A: 좋아요! 그런데 점심은 드셨나요?
B: 아니요. 건물 안에 구내식당이 있나요?
A: 네. 제가 안내해드릴게요.

① 전 아침형 인간인 것 같아요.
② 음악이 마음에 드세요?
③ 소음 수준에 대한 엄격한 규정이 있어요.

어휘 flexible 유연한 cafeteria 구내식당 strict 엄격한 bother 신경 쓰이게 하다

정답 ④

024 밑줄 친 부분에 들어갈 말로 가장 적절한 것은?

> The bully tried to _____ the new student with aggressive behavior.

① coordinate ② negotiate
③ intimidate ④ assist

025 밑줄 친 부분에 들어갈 말로 가장 적절한 것은?

> The company's expenditure has consistently _____ its revenues because of outdated working practices resulting in high labour costs, as well as aged equipment resulting in high operational costs.

① enhanced ② exposed
③ surpassed ④ fabricated

026 밑줄 친 부분에 들어갈 말로 가장 적절한 것은?

> A: I want to go on an international trip for the next vacation. Do you have any suggestions?
> B: How about Europe? Paris or Rome would be amazing.
> A: That's a great idea! I'd love to see the Eiffel Tower in Paris.
> B: Exactly, and in Rome, you should definitely visit the Colosseum.
> A: _____. My summer vacation is only one week long.
> B: In that case, how about Japan or Taiwan? They're closer and still offer wonderful travel experiences.
> A: Sounds good! Tokyo in Japan or Taipei in Taiwan both seem exciting!

① But I'm so into Western culture
② Besides, I'm accompanied by my mother
③ But Europe is too far to travel
④ On top of that, I like adventures

024

해석 그 불량배는 공격적인 행동으로 신입생을 위협하려고 했다.

어휘 bully 불량배 aggressive 공격적인 behavior 행동
coordinate 조정하다 negotiate 협상하다
intimidate 위협하다 assist 돕다

근거

> The bully tried to intimidate the new student with aggressive behavior.

정답 ③

주요 어휘 정리

intimidate 위협하다	assist 돕다
= threaten	= help
browbeat	aid
menace	serve

025

해석 높은 운영비를 초래하는 노후된 장비뿐만 아니라, 높은 인건비를 초래하는 구식의 업무 방법 때문에 회사의 지출은 지속적으로 수입을 초과해 왔다.

어휘 expenditure 지출 consistently 지속적으로 revenue 수입
outdated 구식의 result in ~을 초래[야기]하다
aged 노후된 operational 운영의 enhance 강화하다
expose 드러내다 surpass 초과하다 fabricate 조작하다

근거

> The company's expenditure has consistently surpassed its revenues because of outdated working practices resulting in high labour costs, as well as aged equipment resulting in high operational costs.

정답 ③

주요 어휘 정리

surpass 초과하다, 넘다	fabricate 조작하다
= exceed	= forge
excel	falsify
transcend	feign
outstrip	counterfeit
outdo	
outgo	
outweigh	

026 밑줄 친 부분에 들어갈 말로 가장 적절한 것은?

> A: 다음 휴가 때 해외여행을 가고 싶어요. 제안해 주실 만한 곳 있나요?
> B: 유럽은 어때요? 파리나 로마는 멋질 거예요.
> A: 좋은 생각이네요! 파리에서 에펠탑을 보고 싶어요.
> B: 맞아요, 로마에서는 콜로세움에 꼭 가보셔야 해요.
> A: 하지만 유럽은 여행하기에 너무 멀어요. 제 여름휴가는 겨우 1주일밖에 안 되거든요.
> B: 그렇다면 일본이나 대만은 어떠세요? 더 가깝고 여전히 멋진 여행 경험을 할 수 있어요.
> A: 좋아요! 일본의 도쿄나 대만의 타이베이 둘 다 신날 것 같아요!

① 하지만 저는 서구 문화에 푹 빠져 있어요
② 게다가, 저는 어머니와 동행해요
④ 그뿐 아니라, 저는 모험을 좋아해요

어휘 international trip 해외여행 suggestion 제안
be into ~에 빠지다 accompany 동행하다 on top of ~뿐 아니라
adventure 모험

정답 ③

027 밑줄 친 부분에 들어갈 말로 가장 적절한 것은?

Mila Brooks
Hi, Dr. Johnson. You know my son, Ben?
10:42

Dr. Johnson
Sure. I saw him at family counseling before.
10:43

Mila Brooks
I'm worried about him these days. He wakes up in the middle of the night and won't stop crying.
10:44

Dr. Johnson
I'm sure you've been busy taking care of the baby, and it probably makes Ben feel stressed.
10:45

Mila Brooks
Oh, I don't play with Ben as much as I used to. That could explain his behavior.
10:46

Dr. Johnson
Now, you know what Ben needs.
10:47

Mila Brooks
_____.
10:50

① Right. You can ignore his selfish and rude behavior
② I see. You need to encourage him to fall asleep on his own
③ Yes. I should make time each day to spend with him
④ Certainly. I'll ask him to share his toys with his brother

028 밑줄 친 부분에 들어갈 말로 가장 적절한 것은?

A: Have you noticed any changes in the company's policies lately?
B: Yes, I have. They've updated the remote work policy to allow more flexibility.
A: That's true. I've also heard they're planning to introduce a new performance review system next quarter.
B: Really? In what way do you think the review system will change?
A: It's not certain, but from what I heard, _____.
B: That sounds promising. I'm looking forward to seeing how it works out.

① because of it, our salaries will freeze
② it will be more comprehensive and fair
③ we need to present new performance
④ welfare payments will be gradually reduced

문장 분석 및 해설

027 밑줄 친 부분에 들어갈 말로 가장 적절한 것은?

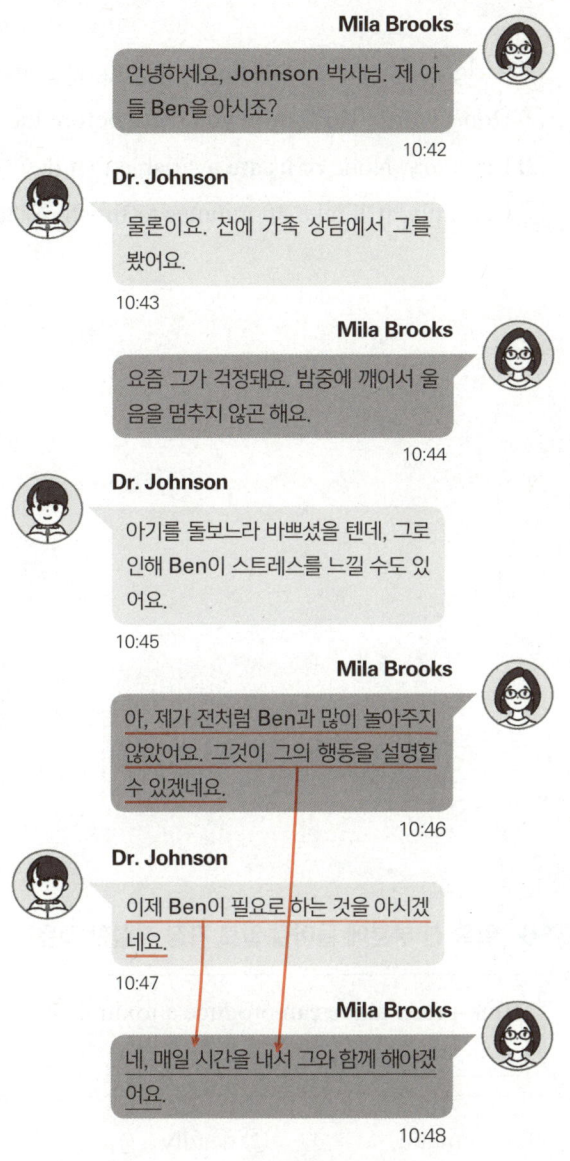

① 맞아요. 그의 이기적이고 무례한 행동은 무시하셔도 돼요
② 그렇군요. 당신은 그가 혼자서 잠들도록 격려해야 해요
④ 물론이죠. 저는 그가 그의 장난감을 남동생과 공유하도록 부탁할게요

어휘 counseling 상담 be busy -ing ~하느라 바쁘다
take care of ~을 돌보다 stressed 스트레스 받는
explain 설명하다 behavior 행동 ignore 무시하다
selfish 이기적인 rude 무례한 encourage 격려하다
fall asleep 잠들다 on one's own 혼자서 share 공유하다

정답 ③

028 밑줄 친 부분에 들어갈 말로 가장 적절한 것은?

A: 최근 회사 정책에 어떤 변화가 있는 것을 눈치채셨나요?
B: 네, 눈치챘어요. 유연성을 높이기 위해 원격 근무 정책을 업데이트했어요.
A: 맞아요. 다음 분기에 새로운 성과 검토 시스템을 도입할 계획이라고도 들었어요.
B: 정말요? 그 검토 시스템이 어떤 식으로 달라질 것 같으세요?
A: 확실하지는 않지만, 제가 들은 바로는, 더 포괄적이고 공정해질 거래요.
B: 조짐이 좋네요. 어떻게 될지 보는 것이 기대가 됩니다.

① 그것 때문에, 우리 봉급이 동결될 거예요
③ 우리는 새로운 퍼포먼스를 선보여야 해요
④ 복지 수당이 점차 줄어들 거예요

어휘 policy 정책 remote work 원격 근무 flexibility 유연성
introduce 도입하다 performance 성과 quarter 분기
salary 봉급 freeze 동결되다 welfare payments 복지 수당
gradually 점차 reduce 줄이다

정답 ②

029 밑줄 친 부분에 들어갈 말로 가장 적절한 것은?

Sarah Stewart: Dad! It's me, Sarah. 10:42

Dad: You seem to get there early. 10:43

Sarah Stewart: Yes, but I've got a big problem. 10:44

Dad: A problem? What is it? 10:45

Sarah Stewart: I just realized that I didn't bring my identification. 10:46

Dad: Oh, do you want me to bring your student ID now? 10:47

Sarah Stewart: That's not possible. I lost my student ID last month at school. 10:48

Dad: Oh, no. Did you ask the test administration about what to do? 10:49

Sarah Stewart: They said I can take the test with my passport instead. 10:50

Dad: _____ 10:51

① Alright. I'll get it and bring it to you right away
② Don't worry. He'll drop you there before the test
③ I'm sorry. None of us are available that day
④ Certainly. It'll take 30 minutes to finish my test

030 밑줄 친 부분에 들어갈 말로 가장 적절한 것은?

> Blue-green algae can produce a toxin that can be _____ to pets.

① enigmatic ② deadly
③ secular   ④ beneficial

029 밑줄 친 부분에 들어갈 말로 가장 적절한 것은?

② 걱정 말아라. 그가 시험 전에 널 내려 줄 거야
③ 미안하다. 우리 중 아무도 그날 시간이 안 돼
④ 물론이지. 내가 시험을 끝내는 데에는 30분이 걸릴 거야

어휘 realize 깨닫다   identification 신원 확인서   student ID 학생증
administration 관리 직원들   passport 여권
drop (어디로 가는 길에) 내려 주다   available 시간이 있는

정답 ①

030

해석 남조류는 반려동물에게 치명적일 수 있는 독소를 만들어낼 수 있다.

어휘 blue-green algae 남조류   toxin 독소   enigmatic 불가사의한
deadly 치명적인   secular 세속적인   beneficial 이로운

근거
> Blue-green algae can produce a toxin that can be deadly to pets.

정답 ②

주요 어휘 정리

enigmatic 수수께끼 같은, 불가사의한
= mysterious
  uncanny
  inscrutable
  cryptic

secular 세속적인, 일상의
= worldly
  everyday
  earthly
  daily
  mundane
  routine

DAY 03   33

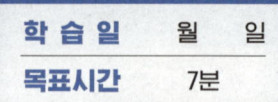

031 밑줄 친 부분에 들어갈 말로 가장 적절한 것은?

> She harbored deep _____ towards her colleague after he took credit for her idea during the meeting.

① caution   ② resentment
③ liberty   ④ struggle

032 밑줄 친 부분에 들어갈 말로 가장 적절한 것은?

> After a lengthy process, the couple was overjoyed by the successful _____ of their baby girl because their family was finally complete. They cherished every moment they spent with her.

① adoption   ② illusion
③ charity   ④ absorption

033 밑줄 친 부분에 들어갈 말로 가장 적절한 것은?

> A: I think we've made good progress on the project today.
> B: Agreed, we've covered a lot of ground.
> A: _____?
> B: Not that I can think of. Everything is going right.
> A: Sounds good! Then let's finish for today.
> B: Great. See you tomorrow!

① Did we receive the shipment of office supplies
② Did we resolve all the issues relate to it
③ Have you finished your performance review
④ Is there anything else we need to finalize

031

해석 그녀는 자기 동료가 회의에서 자기 아이디어에 대한 공을 가로챈 후 그에 대한 깊은 적의를 품었다.

어휘 harbor 품다   colleague 동료
take credit for ~에 대한 공을 가로채다   caution 경고
resentment 적의   liberty 자유   struggle 투쟁

근거

> She harbored deep resentment towards her colleague after he took credit for her idea during the meeting.

정답 ②

주요 어휘 정리
resentment 적의, 분노
= anger
　indignation
　rage
　fury

032

해석 긴 과정 끝에, 그 부부는 마침내 그들의 가족이 완성되었기 때문에 여자 아기를 성공적으로 입양한 것에 매우 기뻐했다. 그들은 그녀와 함께 보내는 모든 순간을 소중히 여겼다.

어휘 lengthy 긴   overjoyed 매우 기뻐하는   complete 완성된
cherish 소중히 여기다   adoption 입양   illusion 착각
charity 자선   absorption 흡수

근거

> After a lengthy process, the couple was overjoyed by the successful adoption of their baby girl because their family was finally complete. They cherished every moment they spent with her.

정답 ①

주요 어휘 정리
illusion 착각, 오해
= myth
　misunderstanding
　delusion
　misconception

033 밑줄 친 부분에 들어갈 말로 가장 적절한 것은?

> A: 오늘 프로젝트 진행이 잘 된 것 같아요.
> B: 동의해요, 저희는 많은 부분을 다루었어요.
> A: 더 마무리해야 할 사항이 있나요?
> B: 제가 생각하기에는 없어요. 모든 것이 제대로 진행되고 있어요.
> A: 좋아요! 그럼, 오늘은 그만합시다.
> B: 좋아요. 내일 뵙겠습니다!

① 사무용품을 배송받았나요
② 그것과 관련된 모든 문제를 해결했나요
③ 성과 검토를 마쳤나요

어휘 cover ground (어떤) 부분을 다루다
receive the shipment 배송을 받다   office supply 사무용품
annual 연간의   performance 성과   finalize 마무리하다

정답 ④

034 밑줄 친 부분에 들어갈 말로 가장 적절한 것은?

> These days, more and more couples opt for small and quiet wedding over overtly _____ wedding so that they can spend more money on their honeymoon or elsewhere.

① malicious ② vigilant
③ inadvertent ④ ostentatious

035 밑줄 친 부분에 들어갈 말로 가장 적절한 것은?

> The scientist found the region to be _____ in natural resources, which could support the local economy.

① abundant ② scarce
③ insufficient ④ humid

036 밑줄 친 부분에 들어갈 말로 가장 적절한 것은?

> A: Hey, did you catch that new movie everyone's talking about?
> B: Yeah, I saw it last weekend. It was pretty good, actually.
> A: Nice! What did you think of the ending?
> B: I liked how they tied everything together, but I didn't expect that twist.
> A: Right? _____.
> B: Definitely. The twist was so good. We should go watch another movie together soon.
> A: Sounds like a plan.

① That's why action-comedies are popular
② The ending was packed with too much action scenes
③ But I'm not sure the twist is necessary
④ It kept me guessing until the last scene

문장 분석 및 해설

034

해석 요즘 점점 더 많은 커플들이 그들의 신혼여행이나 다른 곳에 더 많은 돈을 쓸 수 있도록 공공연히 하는 화려한 결혼식 대신 작고 조용한 결혼식을 선택한다.

어휘 opt 선택하다　overtly 공공연하게 하는　elsewhere 다른 곳
malicious 악의 있는　vigilant 주의하는
inadvertent 고의가 아닌, 우발적인　ostentatious 화려한

근거

> These days, more and more couples opt for small and quiet wedding over overtly ostentatious wedding so that they can spend more money on their honeymoon or elsewhere.

정답 ④

주요 어휘 정리

vigilant 주의하는, 경계하는	ostentatious 화려한, 과시하는
= careful	= showy
watchful	pretentious
heedful	extravagant
cautious	opulent
attentive	boastful
alert	
discreet	
wary	
prudential	
circumspect	

035

해석 그 과학자는 그 지역이 천연자원이 풍부하다는 것을 발견했는데, 그것은 지역 경제를 부양할 수 있었다.

어휘 region 지역　natural resource 천연자원　support 부양하다
abundant 풍부한　scarce 부족한　insufficient 불충분한
humid 습한

근거

> The scientist found the region to be abundant in natural resources, which could support the local economy.

정답 ①

주요 어휘 정리

abundant 풍부한	insufficient 불충분한
= rich	= inadequate
plentiful	deficient
fertile	sparse
bountiful	scarce
ample	

036 밑줄 친 부분에 들어갈 말로 가장 적절한 것은?

> A: 이봐, 사람들이 얘기하는 그 새 영화 봤어?
> B: 응, 지난 주말에 봤어. 사실 꽤나 좋았어.
> A: 좋았어! 결말에 대해 어떻게 생각했어?
> B: 나는 그들이 모든 것을 연결시키는 방식은 마음에 들었지만, 그런 반전은 예상하지 못했어.
> A: 그치? 그게 마지막 장면까지 계속 추측하게 했어.
> B: 확실히 그래. 반전은 너무 훌륭했어. 곧 같이 다른 영화 보러 가자.
> A: 좋은 생각이야.

① 그게 액션 코미디가 인기 있는 이유야
② 마지막 장면은 너무 많은 액션 장면으로 꽉 찼어
③ 그런데 반전이 필요한지 확실하지 않아

어휘 catch 보다　twist 반전　Sounds like a plan. 좋은 생각이야.
be packed with ~으로 꽉 차다　guess 추측하다

정답 ④

037 밑줄 친 부분에 들어갈 말로 가장 적절한 것은?

> A: Are you ready to bowl?
> B: Don't we have to put our names on the computer first?
> A: You're right. I'll put down my regular name. What about you?
> B: I want a funny name for mine. Type Big Bad Bowler.
> A: _____.
> B: Fine, just put my regular name.

① We're ready to start the game
② That name is perfect on you
③ I don't think it fits that many letters
④ That is my type of pseudonym

038 밑줄 친 부분에 들어갈 말로 가장 적절한 것은?

> A: Have you tried that new coffee shop on Main Street?
> B: Yeah, I stopped by yesterday. The espresso was amazing!
> A: Nice! I've been meaning to check it out. What else did they have?
> B: They also had a large selection of baked goods. _____
> A: Really? Then, I'm not coming. I drink coffee always with cookies.

① Why don't we go try some bread?
② But they taste less than appetizing.
③ They have the best patissier ever.
④ Still, it was considered a decent cafe.

037 밑줄 친 부분에 들어갈 말로 가장 적절한 것은?

> A: 볼링 칠 준비 됐니?
> B: 우리 이름을 먼저 컴퓨터에 올려야 하지 않아?
> A: 맞아. 나는 평상시 내 이름을 쓸게. 너는?
> B: 나는 내 이름으로 웃긴 이름을 원해. 크고 무서운 볼링 선수라고 쳐줘.
> A: 그렇게 많은 글자는 맞지 않는 것 같아.
> B: 알겠어, 그냥 내 이름 써줘.

① 우리 게임을 시작할 준비가 됐어
② 그 이름 너한테 딱이다
④ 내가 좋아하는 유형의 가명이야

어휘 bowl 볼링을 치다 regular 평상시의 pseudonym 가명

정답 ③

---

038 밑줄 친 부분에 들어갈 말로 가장 적절한 것은?

> A: 메인 가에 있는 새로운 커피숍에 가봤어?
> B: 응, 어제 들렀어. 에스프레소가 끝내주더라!
> A: 좋았어! 나도 살펴보려고 작정하고 있었어. 그밖에 뭐가 있어?
> B: 다양한 종류의 제과류도 있었어. 그런데 맛이 없었어.
> A: 정말? 그러면, 난 안 갈래. 나는 항상 쿠키와 같이 커피를 마셔.

① 가서 빵을 좀 먹는 게 어때?
③ 거기는 최고의 파티시에가 있어.
④ 그래도, 그곳은 괜찮은 카페로 여겨졌어.

어휘 stop by ~에 들르다 mean 작정하다 check out ~을 살펴보다
a large selection of 다양한 종류의 appetizing 맛있는
patissier 파티시에 decent 괜찮은

정답 ②

039 밑줄 친 부분에 들어갈 말로 가장 적절한 것은?

Diamond Sports Center
Hello, Diamond Sports Center. May I help you?
10:42

Katie Walker
Hello. I'm Katie Walker, and a member of your sports center. I want to know if I can suspend my membership.
10:43

Diamond Sports Center
Okay, You mean you can't come for a while?
10:44

Katie Walker
That's right. I broke my leg yesterday.
10:45

Diamond Sports Center
Oh, I'm sorry. You can put your membership on hold for up to 60 days.
10:46

Katie Walker
_____ The doctor said it would take me at least 3 months to get back to normal.
10:47

Diamond Sports Center
We can bend the rules for you if you submit a medical certificate.
10:48

Katie Walker
Thank you, I'll send it right away.
10:49

① When can I get a full physical examination?
② I'll be able to start again after two months.
③ Why don't you abide by the regulations?
④ I'm sorry, but I need a further suspension.

040 밑줄 친 부분에 들어갈 말로 가장 적절한 것은?

Trade credit insurance has helped _____ many businesses from bad debts and protect them from unpaid invoices caused by customer bankruptcy.

① avert
② infuriate
③ flourish
④ insulate

039 밑줄 친 부분에 들어갈 말로 가장 적절한 것은?

Diamond Sports Center
안녕하세요, Diamond 스포츠 센터입니다. 무엇을 도와드릴까요?

10:42

Katie Walker
안녕하세요. 저는 Katie Walker이고, 귀하의 스포츠 센터 회원입니다. 제 회원권을 중지할 수 있는지 알고 싶어요.
10:43

Diamond Sports Center
네, 당분간 못 오신다는 말씀이신가요?

10:44

Katie Walker
맞아요. 어제 다리가 부러졌거든요.
10:45

Diamond Sports Center
아, 유감이네요. 최대 60일까지 회원권을 연기할 수 있어요.

10:46

Katie Walker
죄송하지만, 추가 연장이 필요해요. 의사 선생님이 제가 정상으로 회복되는 데 적어도 3개월이 걸릴 거라고 하셨거든요.
10:47

Diamond Sports Center
진단서를 제출하시면 편의를 봐 드릴 수 있어요.

10:48

Katie Walker
감사합니다, 당장 보낼게요.
10:49

① 제가 종합 건강 검진을 언제 받을 수 있나요?
② 두 달 뒤에 다시 시작할 수 있을 거예요.
③ 규칙을 지키는 게 어때요?

어휘 suspend 중지하다 membership 회원권 for a while 당분간 break one's leg 다리가 부러지다 put ~ on hold ~을 연기하다 bend the rules 편의를 봐주다 submit 제출하다 medical certificate 진단서 full physical examination 종합 건강 검진 abide by ~을 지키다 regulations 규칙 suspension 연장

정답 ④

040

해석 무역 신용 보험은 수많은 회사들을 불량 채권으로부터 보호하고 그들을 고객 파산으로 인한 미지급 청구서로부터 보호하는 데 도움이 되었다.

어휘 trade 무역 credit 신용 insurance 보험 invoice 청구서 bankruptcy 파산 avert 방지하다 infuriate 극도로 화나게 만들다 flourish 번영하다 insulate 보호하다

근거
> Trade credit insurance has helped insulate many businesses from bad debts and protect them from unpaid invoices caused by customer bankruptcy.

정답 ④

주요 어휘 정리

avert 방지하다, 막다, 피하다
= dodge   head off
  avoid   ward off
  shun   stave off
  evade   steer clear of
  eschew   get around

infuriate 매우 화나게 만들다
= irritate
  incense
  vex
  exasperate
  enrage

flourish 번영하다, 번창하다
= thrive
  prosper

insulate 보호하다
= shield

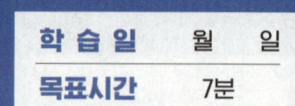

041 밑줄 친 부분에 들어갈 말로 가장 적절한 것은?

The new policy initiatives are expected to _____ significant changes in how the company operates its sustainability programs, potentially reducing carbon emissions by 30% within the next fiscal year.

① cause ② cease
③ suppress ④ shield

042 밑줄 친 부분에 들어갈 말로 가장 적절한 것은?

The doctor was able to _____ the patient's condition and propose a treatment plan after conducting several tests.

① wound ② diagnose
③ bend ④ bruise

043 밑줄 친 부분에 들어갈 말로 가장 적절한 것은?

A: This piece is really unique. It feels like there's a deep story behind it.

B: I agree. The colors and composition are very intriguing.

A: I wonder what the artist's intention was in creating this.

B: Me too. I think this painting visualizes sad emotions.

A: That's deep. I got more curious. _____
_____

B: All right. Wow, my theory was right. It says the artist wanted to express the loneliness of modern life.

A: You're amazing!

① I think you can explain the artist's intentions.
② Why don't we read the artwork description?
③ That's why I feel emotionally connected to you.
④ How about moving on to the next exhibit hall?

041

해석 새로운 정책 계획들은 회사가 지속 가능성 프로그램을 운영하는 방식에 상당한 변화를 초래할 것으로 예상되며, 잠재적으로 다음 회계 연도 내에 탄소 배출량을 30% 감소시킬 것이다.

어휘 policy 정책   initiative 계획   significant 상당한
sustainability 지속 가능성   potentially 잠재적으로
fiscal year 회계 연도   cause 초래하다   cease 중단하다
suppress 진압하다   shield 보호하다

근거

> The new policy initiatives are expected to cause significant changes in how the company operates its sustainability programs, potentially reducing carbon emissions by 30% within the next fiscal year.

정답 ①

주요 어휘 정리

cause 초래하다
= bring about
  lead to
  result in

cease 중단하다
= stop
  end
  discontinue
  halt
  quit

suppress 진압하다
= repress
  control
  quell
  put down
  keep down

042

해석 의사는 여러 차례 검사를 실시한 후에 환자의 상태를 진단하고 치료계획을 제안할 수 있었다.

어휘 patient 환자   condition 상태   conduct 실시하다
wound 부상을 입히다   diagnose 진단하다   bend 구부리다
bruise 타박상을 입히다

근거

> The doctor was able to diagnose the patient's condition and propose a treatment plan after conducting several tests.

정답 ②

주요 어휘 정리

diagnose 진단하다
= identify
  determine
  detect

wound 부상을 입히다
= hurt
  injure

043 밑줄 친 부분에 들어갈 말로 가장 적절한 것은?

> A: 이 작품 정말 독특하네요. 이면에 깊은 이야기가 담겨 있는 것 같아요.
> B: 맞아요. 색감과 구도가 아주 흥미로워요.
> A: 작가가 어떤 의도로 이 작품을 만들었는지 궁금해지네요.
> B: 저도요. 이 그림은 슬픈 감정을 시각화한 것 같아요.
> A: 심오하네요. 더 궁금해졌어요. 작품 해설을 읽어보는 게 어때요?
> B: 좋아요. 와, 제 생각이 맞았어요. 화가가 현대 생활의 외로움을 표현하려 했다고 쓰여 있어요.
> A: 정말 대단하세요!

① 당신이 화가의 의도를 설명해줄 수 있을 것 같아요.
③ 그런 이유로 저는 정서적으로 당신과 연결된 기분이에요.
④ 다음 전시실로 넘어가는 게 어때요?

어휘 composition 구도   intriguing 아주 흥미로운
visualize 시각화하다   emotion 감정   curious 궁금한
theory 생각   loneliness 외로움   intention 의도
description 해설   move on to ~로 넘어가다

정답 ②

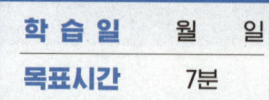

044 밑줄 친 부분에 들어갈 말로 가장 적절한 것은?

> Even after achieving something and ascending somewhere in life, it is human nature to _____ better things as well as higher places.

① advocate   ② yearn
③ compensate   ④ blame

045 밑줄 친 부분에 들어갈 말로 가장 적절한 것은?

> At one point, she experienced a serious injury that could have _____ her career.

① enhanced   ② jeopardized
③ maintained   ④ endorsed

046 밑줄 친 부분에 들어갈 말로 가장 적절한 것은?

> A: I can't believe the discounted price of this sweater. I think it's a good bargain.
> B: But you can only get the discount if you have the coupon downloaded through the website.
> A: Oh, I see. All I need to do is to go to the website and download a coupon?
> B: That's right. But to download the coupon, you need to sign up as a member first.
> A: I got it. _____
> B: Sure. Let me show you how to sign up.

① So much for today.
② Which way should we go?
③ Can I do that right now on my cell-phone?
④ Can you show me the way to the information desk?

044

해석 인생에서 무언가를 성취하고 어딘가에 오른 뒤에도, 더 높은 위치뿐만 아니라 더 좋은 것을 갈망하는 것은 인간의 본능이다.

어휘 achieve 성취하다　ascend 오르다　nature 본능
advocate 지지하다　yearn 갈망하다　compensate 보상하다
blame 탓하다

근거

> Even after achieving something and ascending somewhere in life, it is human nature to yearn better things as well as higher places.

정답 ②

주요 어휘 정리

yearn 갈망하다	blame 탓하다
= long	= criticize
crave	condemn
desire	denounce
want	
covet	

045

해석 한때 그녀는 자기 경력을 위태롭게 할 수도 있었던 심각한 부상을 경험했다.

어휘 serious 심각한　injury 부상　career 경력　enhance 향상시키다
jeopardized 위태롭게 하다　maintain 유지하다
endorse 지지하다

근거

> At one point, she experienced a serious injury that could have jeopardized her career.

정답 ②

주요 어휘 정리

jeopardize 위태롭게 하다	endorse 지지하다
= threaten	= support
endanger	advocate
imperil	uphold
risk	champion

046

A: 이 스웨터의 할인 가격을 믿을 수가 없어요. 특가품 같아요.
B: 하지만 홈페이지를 통해 쿠폰을 다운로드 받아야만 할인을 받으실 수 있어요.
A: 아, 그렇군요. 홈페이지에 들어가서 쿠폰을 다운로드하기만 하면 되나요?
B: 맞습니다. 하지만 쿠폰을 다운로드하려면 회원가입을 먼저 하셔야 해요.
A: 알겠습니다. 지금 바로 제 핸드폰으로 해도 되나요?
B: 네. 제가 가입하는 법을 알려드릴게요.

① 오늘은 이쯤하고 끝냅시다.
② 우리가 어느 길로 가야 하죠?
④ 안내 데스크로 가는 길 좀 알려주시겠어요?

어휘 good bargain 특가품　sign up 가입하다

정답 ③

047 밑줄 친 부분에 들어갈 말로 가장 적절한 것은?

Emily Johnson: Honey, do you know where the camera is? 10:42

Mark Johnson: I put it on the desk. Why do you need it? 10:43

Emily Johnson: It's for Kevin's school concert. 10:44

Mark Johnson: Oh, right! It's tomorrow! 10:45

Emily Johnson: Didn't you say you have an important meeting tomorrow? 10:46

Mark Johnson: Yes, I did. It was impossible to reschedule it. 10:47

Emily Johnson: That's okay. I'll record his performance so you won't miss a thing. 10:48

Mark Johnson: Thanks, if the meeting ends early, I might be able to be there by four. 10:49

Emily Johnson: _____ 10:50

Mark Johnson: At least, I can pick you guys up and go home together. 10:51

① Great. We need a ride to the concert hall.
② Right. I'll buy a new camera this afternoon.
③ What for? The concert will be over by then.
④ No way! Postpone the meeting for our son.

048 밑줄 친 부분에 들어갈 말로 가장 적절한 것은?

A: Are you managing your blood sugar well these days?
B: Yes, I'm paying more attention to my diet. I'm especially trying to cut down on carbs.
A: That's great. Are you exercising regularly?
B: Yes, I've been walking for 30 minutes every day. It really helps with blood sugar control.
A: Absolutely, exercise is really important. Are you taking your medication regularly?
B: _____.
A: You're doing a good job. Keep it up, and things will keep improving!

① I've been forgetting to take it most days.
② I make sure to take it as my doctor prescribed
③ I take it whenever I feel like it
④ You are doing things to boost your immunity

047 밑줄 친 부분에 들어갈 말로 가장 적절한 것은?

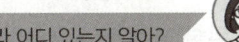
여보, 카메라 어디 있는지 알아?
10:42

Mark Johnson
책상 위에 올려놨어. 왜 그게 필요한 거야?
10:43

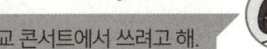
Kevin의 학교 콘서트에서 쓰려고 해.
10:44

Mark Johnson
아, 맞아! 내일이네!
10:45

Emily Johnson
내일 중요한 회의가 있다고 하지 않았어?
10:46

Mark Johnson
응, 그랬지. 일정을 변경하는 건 불가능했어.
10:47

Emily Johnson
괜찮아. 내가 그의 공연을 녹화해서 당신이 하나도 놓치지 않도록 할게.
10:48

Mark Johnson
고마워. 회의가 일찍 끝나면 4시까지 그곳에 갈 수 있을 지도 몰라.
10:49

Emily Johnson
뭐하러? 콘서트는 그때쯤 끝날 텐데.
10:50

Mark Johnson
<u>적어도, 당신이랑 Kevin을 차에 태우고 집에 같이 갈 수는 있잖아.</u>
10:51

① 좋아. 우린 콘서트장으로 갈 차편이 필요해.
② 맞아. 나는 오늘 오후에 새 카메라를 살 거야.
④ 안 돼! 우리 아들을 위해서 회의를 연기해.

어휘 reschedule 일정을 변경하다 record 녹화하다
performance 공연 pick up ~을 태우다
need a ride 차편이 필요하다 postpone 미루다

정답 ③

---

048 밑줄 친 부분에 들어갈 말로 가장 적절한 것은?

A: 요즘 혈당은 잘 관리하고 있어요?
B: 네, 식단에 더 신경 쓰고 있어요. 특히 탄수화물 식품을 줄이려고 노력 중이에요.
A: 잘하고 있네요. 운동은 규칙적으로 하고 있어요?
B: 네, 하루에 30분씩 걷기를 하고 있어요. 혈당 조절에 정말 도움이 돼요.
A: 맞아요, 운동은 정말 중요하죠. <u>약은 규칙적으로 먹고 있죠?</u>
B: <u>의사 선생님께서 처방해 주신 대로 챙겨 먹고 있어요.</u>
A: 잘하고 있어요. 꾸준히 하면, 계속해서 좋아질 거예요!

① 거의 매일 그것을 섭취하는 것을 잊었어요
③ 제가 먹고 싶을 때마다 먹어요
④ 당신은 면역력을 높이기 위해 여러 가지 일을 하고 있어요

어휘 manage 관리하다 blood sugar 혈당
pay attention to ~에 신경을 쓰다 diet 식단
cut down on ~을 줄이다 carbs 탄수화물 식품
exercise 운동하다 regularly 규칙적으로 control 조절
medication 약 Keep it up. 꾸준히 해요. most days 거의 매일
prescribe 처방하다 boost 높이다 immunity 면역력

정답 ②

DAY 05

049 밑줄 친 부분에 들어갈 말로 가장 적절한 것은?

Hannah Baker: Andrew, did you choose a topic for the English essay? 10:42

Andrew Scott: I did. 10:43

Hannah Baker: Have you started writing it? 10:44

Andrew Scott: Not yet. I usually have a hard time making logical arguments for my essays. Do you have any suggestions? 10:45

Hannah Baker: Well, I read a lot of newspaper articles. If you read persuasive articles like editorials, you can see how the arguments are developed. 10:46

Andrew Scott: That makes sense to me. Maybe I should give it a try. 10:47

Hannah Baker: _____. 10:48

Andrew Scott: Thank you. That'll be very helpful for me to start reading editorials. 10:49

① Not all information written on articles is true
② I will send you links to the relevant articles
③ You had better find out references for yourself
④ It wouldn't hurt you to write in your own words

050 밑줄 친 부분에 들어갈 말로 가장 적절한 것은?

In order to _____ the financial crisis that is likely to unfold after retirement, people should be proactive and prepared for the life after retirement.

① overlook
② complicate
③ avoid
④ exacerbate

049 밑줄 친 부분에 들어갈 말로 가장 적절한 것은?

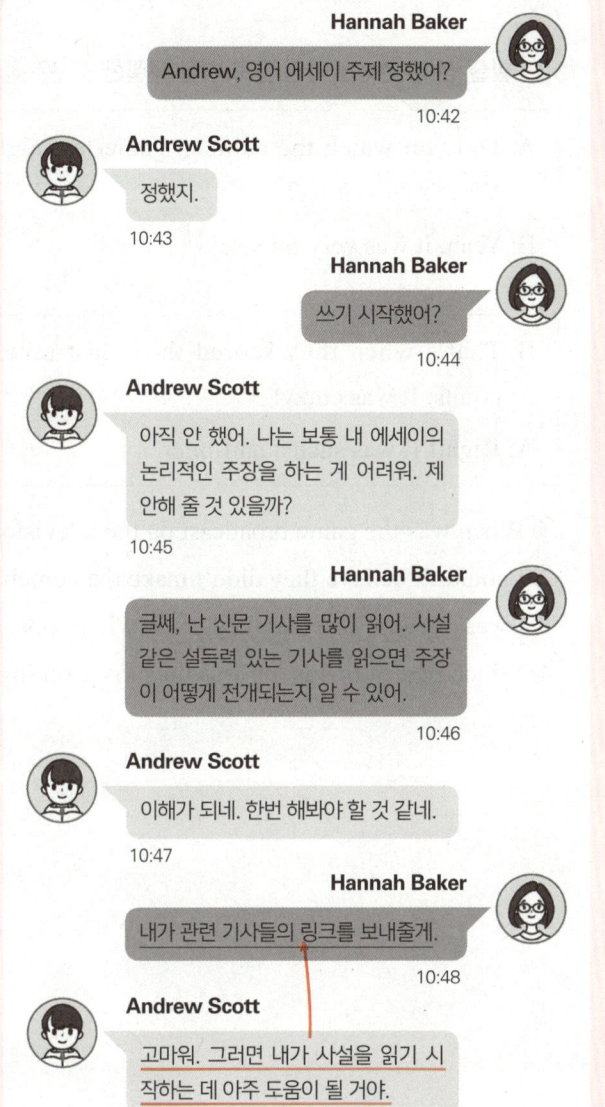

① 기사에 쓰인 모든 정보가 사실인 건 아니야
③ 네가 직접 참고 자료를 찾는 게 좋아
④ 너만의 표현으로 글을 써서 해 될 건 없어

어휘 have a hard time -ing ~하는 것이 어렵다   argument 주장
suggestion 제안   article 기사   persuasive 설득력 있는
editorial 사설   develop 전개하다   make sense 이해하기 쉽다
give it a try 한번 해보다   relevant 관련이 있는
reference 참고 자료   in one's own words ~만의 표현으로

정답 ②

050

해석 은퇴 후 일어날 가능성이 있는 재정 위기를 피하기 위해서, 사람들은 사전 대책을 강구하고 은퇴 후의 삶에 대해 준비해야 한다.

어휘 financial 재정의   crisis 위기   unfold 일어나다   retirement 은퇴
proactive 사전 대책을 강구하는   overlook 간과하다
complicate 복잡하게 만들다   avoid 피하다
exacerbate 악화시키다

근거

> In order to avoid the financial crisis that is likely to unfold after retirement, people should be proactive and prepared for the life after retirement.

정답 ③

주요 어휘 정리

avoid 피하다	exacerbate 악화시키다 ↔	alleviate 완화하다
= shun	= aggravate	= reduce
avert	make worse	relieve
eschew	worsen	relax
evade		soothe
circumvent		calm

overlook 간과하다, 무시하다
= condone
 ignore

051 밑줄 친 부분에 들어갈 말로 가장 적절한 것은?

> She experienced extreme _____ after working long hours without a break.

① obesity ② vitality
③ fatigue ④ nutrition

052 밑줄 친 부분에 들어갈 말로 가장 적절한 것은?

> On one hand, I know I could be better with money. But on the other, I never want to be as _____ as my partner who is an extreme saver.

① lively ② frugal
③ prodigal ④ conscientious

053 밑줄 친 부분에 들어갈 말로 가장 적절한 것은?

> A: Did you watch the national game last night? Wasn't it exciting?
> B: Yeah, it was very intense!
> A: _____
> B: That's when they scored those last-minute points. It was crazy!
> A: Right! It was such a nail-biter.

① When was the game broadcast on the television?
② I couldn't believe they didn't make the comeback.
③ I was not sure whether they could win or not.
④ Which part of that game was the most exciting?

051

해석 그녀는 쉬지 않고 장시간 근무한 끝에 극심한 피로를 느꼈다.

어휘 extreme 극심한   without a break 쉬지 않고   obesity 비만
vitality 활력   fatigue 피로   nutrition 영양

근거

> She experienced extreme fatigue after working long hours without a break.

정답 ③

주요 어휘 정리
fatigue 피로
= exhaustion
  tiredness
  weariness

052

해석 한편으로, 나는 내가 돈이 있으면 더 나아질 수 있다는 것을 안다. 그러나 다른 한편으로는, 나는 절대 지나친 절약가인 내 배우자처럼 절약하고 싶지 않다.

어휘 extreme 지나친   lively 활기 넘치는   frugal 절약하는
prodigal 사치스러운   conscientious 양심적인

근거

> On one hand, I know I could be better with money. But on the other, I never want to be as frugal as my partner who is an extreme saver.

정답 ②

주요 어휘 정리
frugal 절약하는, 검소한   prodigal 사치스러운, 낭비하는
= thrifty   = wasteful
  economical   lavish
                                   extravagant
                                   luxurious

053 밑줄 친 부분에 들어갈 말로 가장 적절한 것은?

> A: 어젯밤 그 경기 봤어? 재미있지 않았어?
> B: 응, 정말 강렬한 경기였어!
> A: 그 경기의 어느 부분이 제일 재미있었어?
> B: 바로 그들이 마지막 순간에 점수를 넣었을 때였어. 엄청났어!
> A: 맞아. 정말 손에 땀을 쥐게 했어.

① 그 경기가 언제 텔레비전으로 중계되었어?
② 그들이 열세를 만회하지 못했다니 믿을 수가 없었어.
③ 나는 그들이 이길지 질지 확신하지 못했어.

어휘 intense 격렬한   score 득점하다   last-minute 마지막 순간의
nail-biter 손에 땀을 쥐게 하는 경기[영화, 이야기]
broadcast 중계하다   comeback 열세의 만회

정답 ④

DAY 06

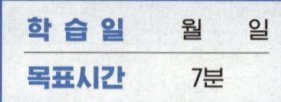

054 밑줄 친 부분에 들어갈 말로 가장 적절한 것은?

> A: Wow, this spaghetti is amazing!
> B: I'm glad you like it! I thought I'd experiment a bit with the sauce. I'm glad it turned out well.
> A: _____
> B: Sure! There's plenty left. Help yourself. How was your day?
> A: Thanks! My day was busy, but now that I'm eating this delicious meal, I feel much better.
> B: I'm glad to hear that! Let me know if you need anything else.

① How much pasta did you make at once?
② Would you have sauce left for later?
③ I skipped lunch, so can I have some more?
④ Can I help you with the dishes after dinner?

055 밑줄 친 부분에 들어갈 말로 가장 적절한 것은?

> In her first Instagram post, the movie star would sing, dance, pose her way through the streets of New York, and _____ her glamorous outfit and unbothered attitude. Big crowds gathered wherever she showed up.

① conceal   ② shrink
③ flatter   ④ brag

056 밑줄 친 부분에 들어갈 말로 가장 적절한 것은?

> One of the most challenging things about working from home is trying to avoid falling into a(n) _____ lifestyle. When someone works from home, he or she may only need to take a few steps to get to their desk or to the kitchen for lunch.

① sedentary   ② solitary
③ peculiar   ④ rudimentary

문장 분석 및 해설

054 밑줄 친 부분에 들어갈 말로 가장 적절한 것은?

> A: 와, 이 스파게티 정말 끝내줘요!
> B: 좋아하시니 다행이네요! 소스를 조금 실험해 볼까 했거든요. 잘 나와서 다행이네요.
> A: 제가 점심을 걸렀는데, 좀 더 먹어도 되나요?
> B: 물론이죠! 많이 남았어요. 많이 드세요. 오늘 하루는 어떠셨나요?
> A: 고마워요! 하루는 바빴는데 이렇게 맛있는 걸 먹으니 기분이 훨씬 좋아졌어요.
> B: 다행이네요! 더 필요한 거 있으시면 말씀해주세요.

① 파스타를 한 번에 얼마나 많이 만드셨나요?
② 나중을 위해서 소스를 남겨두시겠어요?
④ 저녁 식사 후에 설거지를 도와드릴까요?

어휘 experiment with ~을 실험하다 turn out (결과가) 나오다
Help yourself. 많이 드세요. now that ~하니까 at once 한 번에
noodle 국수 skip 거르다 help with the dishes 설거지를 돕다

정답 ③

055

해석 그녀의 첫 번째 인스타그램 게시물에서 그 스타 영화배우는 노래하고 춤을 추고 포즈를 취하며 뉴욕 거리를 누비며 화려한 의상과 신경 쓰지 않는 태도를 뽐냈다. 그녀가 나타나는 곳마다 많은 군중이 모였다.

어휘 post 게시물
pose one's way through 포즈를 취하며 ~ 전역을 돌아다니다
glamorous 화려한 outfit 의상 unbothered 신경 쓰지 않는
conceal 감추다 shrink 수축시키다 flatter 우쭐하게 하다
brag 뽐내다

근거

> In her first Instagram post, the movie star would sing, dance, pose her way through the streets of New York, and brag her glamorous outfit and unbothered attitude. Big crowds gathered wherever she showed up.

정답 ④

주요 어휘 정리

conceal 숨기다
= hide
  veil

brag 자랑하다, 과시하다
= boast
  show off

flatter 아첨하다, 우쭐하게 하다
= make up to
  play up to
  butter up
  praise

056

해석 재택근무를 하면서 가장 어려운 것 중 하나는 주로 앉아서 하는 생활방식에 빠지지 않으려고 노력하는 것이다. 집에서 일할 때, 그 또는 그녀는 점심을 먹으려고 책상이나 부엌으로 가기 위해 몇 걸음만 걸으면 될 것이다.

어휘 challenging 어려운 fall into ~에 빠지다
sedentary 주로 앉아서 하는 solitary 혼자의 peculiar 이상한
rudimentary 가장 기본적인

근거

> One of the most challenging things about working from home is trying to avoid falling into a(n) sedentary lifestyle. When someone works from home, he or she may only need to take a few steps to get to their desk or to the kitchen for lunch.

정답 ①

주요 어휘 정리

sedentary	solitary	↔ gregarious
주로 앉아서 하는	혼자의, 혼자서 하는	사교적인
= inactive lethargic		
inert dormant		
static torpid		
stagnant indolent		
sluggish listless		

peculiar 이상한
= strange weird
  odd eerie
  queer idiosyncratic
  bizarre uncanny
  eccentric out in left field

rudimentary 가장 기본적인
= basic
  cardinal
  elementary
  fundamental

057 밑줄 친 부분에 들어갈 말로 가장 적절한 것은?

> A: Hello, I want to check out. Here is my room key.
> B: Just one second, sir, and I'll give you your receipt. Here you go.
> A: Thank you very much.
> B: Sir, _____
> A: This hotel could use some insecticide, but my time in New York was thoroughly delightful.
> B: Thank you for your honesty. I assure you there will be no insects next time.

① I apologize for your inconvenience you've experienced.
② you have unpaid fees for extra room service.
③ what is your first priority in choosing the hotel?
④ how did you enjoy your stay at New York Hotel?

058 밑줄 친 부분에 들어갈 말로 가장 적절한 것은?

> A: I'm thinking of redecorating my living room. Any suggestions?
> B: How about _____?
> A: That's a good idea. I've been looking for ways to brighten up the space.
> B: You could also consider adding some indoor plants for a fresh look.
> A: I like that idea. Thanks for the tips!

① adopting a companion dog
② moving to a quieter place
③ adding some new colorful throw pillows and rugs
④ making a mini garden by the window

문장 분석 및 해설

057 밑줄 친 부분에 들어갈 말로 가장 적절한 것은?

> A: 안녕하세요, 체크아웃하려고 합니다. 여기 제 방 열쇠입니다.
> B: 잠시만요, 손님, 영수증 드리겠습니다. 여기 있습니다.
> A: 감사합니다.
> B: 손님, 뉴욕호텔에서의 숙박은 어땠나요?
> A: 이 호텔은 살충제를 사용해야겠지만, 뉴욕에서 보낸 시간은 대단히 마음에 들었습니다.
> B: 솔직하게 말씀해 주셔서 감사합니다. 다음번에는 벌레가 없을 것이라고 보장합니다.

① 불편을 끼쳐드려 죄송합니다.
② 추가 룸서비스에 대한 미납금액이 있습니다.
③ 호텔을 선택할 때에 가장 우선순위가 무엇입니까?

어휘 insecticide 살충제   thoroughly 대단히   delightful 마음에 드는   assure 보장하다   unpaid 미납된   priority 우선순위

정답 ④

---

058 밑줄 친 부분에 들어갈 말로 가장 적절한 것은?

> A: 거실을 새로 장식하려고 생각 중이야. 의견 있어?
> B: 새로운 다채로운 쿠션과 깔개를 더하는 건 어때?
> A: 그거 좋은 생각인데. 공간을 환하게 할 방법을 찾는 중이었어.
> B: 산뜻한 모습을 보려면 실내용 식물을 추가하는 것도 고려해 볼 수 있어.
> A: 그 생각 마음에 드네. 조언 주어서 고마워!

① 반려견을 입양하는 건
② 더 조용한 곳으로 이사하는 건
④ 창 옆에 미니 정원을 만드는 건

어휘 redecorate 실내 장식을 새로 하다   brighten 환하게 하다   adopt 입양하다   companion dog 반려견   throw pillow 쿠션   rug 깔개

정답 ③

059 밑줄 친 부분에 들어갈 말로 가장 적절한 것은?

Ella Blake
Hello! I'd like to order some macarons for this afternoon. Is that possible?
10:42

Dessert Shop
Hello! Yes, of course. What flavors would you like?
10:43

Ella Blake
I'd like 3 vanilla, 3 chocolate, 3 raspberry, and 3 pistachio, please.
10:44

Dessert Shop
Sure, that's 12 macarons in total. _____?
10:45

Ella Blake
Yes, could you please package them as a gift? And can I pick them up around 3 PM?
10:46

Dessert Shop
Got it. I'll prepare them with gift packaging. They'll be ready by 3 PM. Thank you!
10:47

Ella Blake
Thank you!
10:48

① Could you share any feedback
② Are there any other flavors you want to try
③ Are there any dietary restrictions or allergies
④ Do you have any specific requests on this order

060 밑줄 친 부분에 들어갈 말로 가장 적절한 것은??

A good barista, or a coffee professional has to have a _____ sense of taste as well as smell to distinguish between different flavors and aromas.

① blunt ② spare
③ clumsy ④ keen

059 밑줄 친 부분에 들어갈 말로 가장 적절한 것은?

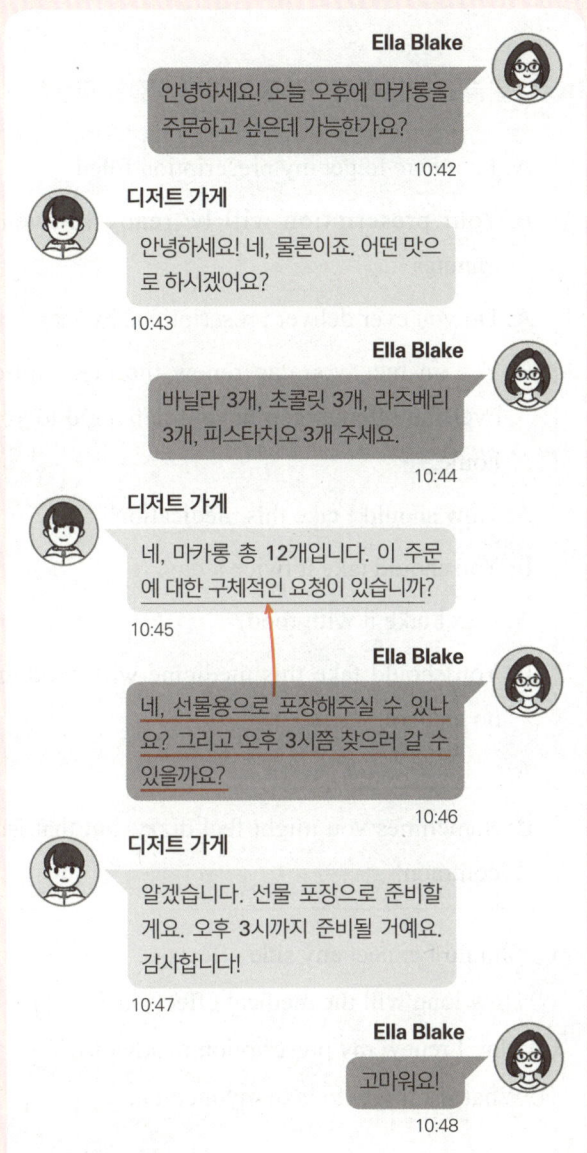

① 공유해주실 피드백이 있으신가요
② 먹어보고 싶은 다른 맛이 있나요
③ 식이 제한이나 알레르기가 있나요

어휘 flavor 맛   package 포장하다   pick up 찾아가다
Got it. 알겠습니다.   dietary 식이의   restriction 제한
allergy 알레르기   specific 구체적인   request 요청

정답 ④

060

해석 훌륭한 바리스타, 즉 커피 전문가는 다양한 맛과 향을 구분하기 위해 예민한 후각 뿐 아니라 미각도 가지고 있어야만 한다.

어휘 coffee professional 커피 전문가   distinguish 구분하다
aroma 향   blunt 무딘   spare 여분의, 남는, 여가의; 아끼다
clumsy 서툰   keen 예민한

근거
A good barista, or a coffee professional has to have a keen sense of taste as well as smell to distinguish between different flavors and aromas.

정답 ④

주요 어휘 정리
blunt 무딘 ↔ keen 예민한 / 날카로운
= dull   = sensitive   = sharp
                              acute

clumsy 서툰
= poor
  inept
  maladroit
  all thumbs

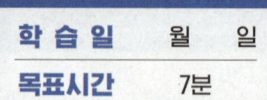

061 밑줄 친 부분에 들어갈 말로 가장 적절한 것은?

The war prisoners were imprisoned in 10 _____ camps, later to be moved to permanent relocation centers.

① perpetual ② temporary
③ severe ④ valid

062 밑줄 친 부분에 들어갈 말로 가장 적절한 것은?

The sight of beggars on city streets and the _____ of the homeless may inspire sympathy, for the same reason.

① charity ② blunder
③ plight ④ dearth

063 밑줄 친 부분에 들어갈 말로 가장 적절한 것은?

A: I am here to get my prescription filled.
B: Your prescription will be ready in twenty minutes.
A: Do you ever deliver prescriptions by mail?
B: Yes, in fact, you can renew the prescription over the Internet and have it delivered to your home.
A: How should I take this medication?
B; You should take it twice a day.
A: Can I take it with food?
B: You should take this medicine with food and no alcohol.
A: _____?
B: Sometimes you might feel dizzy, but that isn't common.

① Should I expect any side effects
② How long will the medical effects last
③ May I renew my prescription in advance
④ What if I forget to take my medicine

061

해석 전쟁 포로들은 10개의 임시 수용소에 수감되었고, 이후 영구적인 강제 수용 센터로 옮겨졌다.

어휘 prisoner 포로 imprison 수감하다 relocation 강제 수용
permanent 영구적인 perpetual 끊임없이 계속되는
temporary 임시의 severe 엄격한 valid 유효한

근거
> The war prisoners were imprisoned in 10 temporary camps, later to be moved to permanent relocation centers.

정답 ②

주요 어휘 정리

temporary 임시의
= provisional   ephemeral
  momentary   fleeting
  transient
  transitory
  tentative
  evanescent

perpetual 영원한
= permanent
  perennial
  persistent
  eternal
  everlasting
  incessant
  ceaseless
  unceasing
  lasting

062

해석 도시 거리의 거지들의 모습과 노숙자의 곤경은 같은 이유로 동정심을 불러일으키는 것 같다.

어휘 beggar 거지 homeless 노숙자, 집이 없는 사람
inspire 불러일으키다 charity 자선, 자비 blunder 실수
plight 곤경 dearth 부족

근거
> The sight of beggars on city streets and the plight of the homeless may inspire sympathy, for the same reason.

정답 ③

주요 어휘 정리

plight 역경, 곤경
= trouble
  difficulty
  dilemma
  difficult situation
  predicament
  quandary

blunder 실수
= mistake
  gaffe
  fault
  error

dearth 부족, 결핍
= lack
  insufficiency
  shortage
  deficiency
  scarcity

063 밑줄 친 부분에 들어갈 말로 가장 적절한 것은?

> A: 처방 약을 받으러 왔어요.
> B: 20분 안에 처방 약이 준비될 거예요.
> A: 혹시 우편으로 처방 약을 배달해주신 적이 있나요?
> B: 네, 사실 이 처방전을 인터넷으로 갱신해서 약을 집으로 배송 받으실 수 있습니다.
> A: 이 약은 어떻게 먹어야 하나요?
> B: 하루에 두 번 드셔야 합니다.
> A: 음식이랑 같이 먹어도 되나요?
> B: 이 약은 음식과 함께 드셔야 하고 술은 드시면 안 됩니다.
> A: 부작용을 예상해야 하나요?
> B: 가끔 어지러울 때도 있지만, 그런 경우는 흔하지 않아요.

② 의료 효과는 얼마나 오래 지속되나요
③ 미리 처방전을 갱신해도 될까요
④ 약 먹는 것을 잊으면 어떻게 하죠

어휘 prescription 처방 약 renew 갱신하다 medication 약
dizzy 어지러운 common 흔한 side effect 부작용
last 지속되다 in advance 미리

정답 ①

064 빈칸에 들어갈 말로 가장 적절한 것은?

With pouring rain that didn't seem to _____ anytime soon, the couple went around knocking doors, asking for shelter.

① diminish   ② increase
③ amplify   ④ worsen

065 밑줄 친 부분에 들어갈 말로 가장 적절한 것은?

The new hotel boasts of its _____ outdoor facilities such as the outdoor tennis courts, a spacious well-lit patio and a teardrop-shaped swimming pool.

① fragile   ② surprised
③ impeccable   ④ worthless

066 밑줄 친 부분에 들어갈 말로 가장 적절한 것은?

A: Are you hurt? You have a bruised eye. Did you get into a fight or something?
B: My brother did it to me! I can't stand it any more. He's got to pay for it.
A: _____
B: Well, actually, I drove his car without his permission and crashed with another car.
A: You really did so? No wonder why he hit you.
B: But the damages are barely noticeable! It was just a fender bender!

① Do you think that doesn't make him a bad person?
② He wouldn't do such a thing without a good reason.
③ Who on earth did give you a permission to hit him?
④ I have heard what happened between you two.

064

해석 금방 약해질 것 같지 않은 장대비로 인해, 그 부부는 주변의 문을 두드리며 잠시 비 피할 곳을 요청했다.

어휘 shelter 잠시 비를 피하는 곳, 대피소　diminish 약해지다
increase 증가하다　amplify 확대되다　worsen 악화되다

근거

> With pouring rain that didn't seem to diminish anytime soon, the couple went around knocking doors, asking for shelter.

정답 ①

주요 어휘 정리
diminish 약해지다, 줄어들다
= weaken
　decrease
　dwindle
　decline
　wane

065

해석 새 호텔은 야외 테니스 코트, 햇빛이 잘 드는 널찍한 테라스, 그리고 눈물방울 모양의 수영장과 같은 완벽한 야외 시설을 자랑한다.

어휘 boast 자랑하다　spacious 널찍한　fragile 약한
surprised 놀란(cf. surprising 놀라운)　impeccable 완벽한
worthless 가치 없는, 쓸모없는

근거

> The new hotel boasts of its impeccable outdoor facilities such as the outdoor tennis courts, a spacious well-lit patio and a teardrop-shaped swimming pool.

정답 ③

주요 어휘 정리
fragile 약한, 깨지기 쉬운　　impeccable 완벽한, 무결점의
= brittle　　　　　　　　　　= faultless
　breakable　　　　　　　　　flawless
　feeble　　　　　　　　　　　immaculate
　frail　　　　　　　　　　　　unblemished
　weak　　　　　　　　　　　perfect

066 밑줄 친 부분에 들어갈 말로 가장 적절한 것은?

> A: 너 다쳤니? 눈이 멍들었네. 싸움에 휘말리거나 뭐 그런 거야?
> B: 우리 형이 그랬어! 더는 못 참겠어. 형도 당해봐야 해.
> A: 그가 정당한 이유 없이 그랬을 리가 없는데.
> B: 음, 사실, 내가 형 차를 허락 없이 몰고 나갔다 다른 차량을 박긴 했지.
> A: 너가 정말 그랬어? 형이 왜 널 때렸는지 알 만하다.
> B: 하지만 손상은 눈에 띄지도 않아. 그건 단순히 접촉 사고였다고!

① 그렇다고 그가 나쁜 사람이 되는 것은 아니라고 생각해?
③ 대체 누가 너에게 그를 때려도 된다고 허락한 거야?
④ 너희 둘 사이에 무슨 일이 있었는지 들었어.

어휘 bruised 멍든　stand 참다　pay for (보복을) 당하다
permission 허락　damage 손상　noticeable 눈에 띄는
fender bender 접촉 사고,

정답 ②

067 밑줄 친 부분에 들어갈 말로 가장 적절한 것은?

Customer: Hi there! I'm interested in hiring a party planner. Can you help me? 10:42

Party Planner: Hello! Of course, I'd be happy to assist. What type of event are you planning? 10:43

Customer: I'm organizing a graduation party for my daughter. We're expecting around 50 guests. 10:44

Party Planner: Wonderful! Do you have a budget in mind for the event? 10:45

Customer: We're looking to stay around $5,000. 10:46

Party Planner: _____? 10:47

Customer: We're aiming for preferably a venue with outdoor space. 10:48

Party Planner: Understood. I'll create a package tailored to your preference. 10:49

Customer: Thank you so much! 10:50

① Do you have any specific decoration requirements
② Are there any particular preferences for food
③ Where would you like the party to take place
④ Do you have a specific atmosphere in mind

068 밑줄 친 부분에 들어갈 말로 가장 적절한 것은?

A: Have you been following the news lately?
B: Yeah, it's been pretty hectic. There is so much happening in the world.
A: I know, it's hard to keep up sometimes. _____
B: The new environmental policies seem promising. It's about time we took action.
A: Absolutely. I hope they make a real difference.

① Have you seen the news on polar bears?
② Have you participated in ecology campaigns?
③ What are your thoughts on corporal punishment?
④ Any headlines that caught your attention?

067 밑줄 친 부분에 들어갈 말로 가장 적절한 것은?

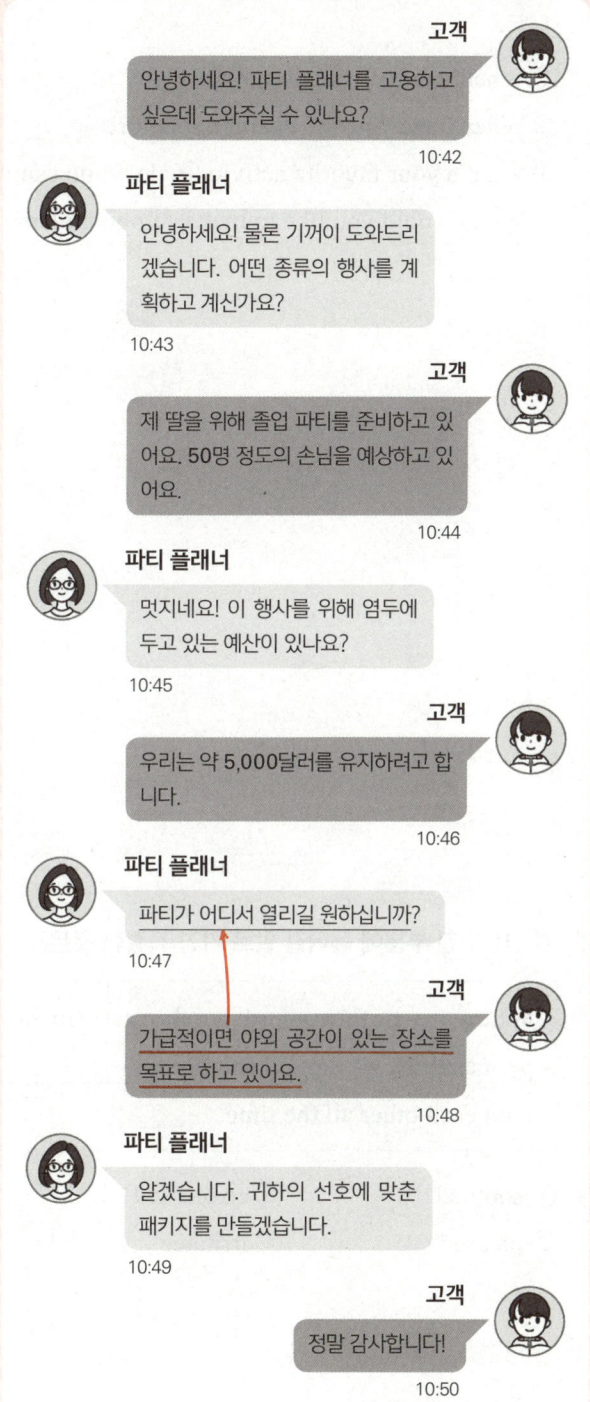

① 특정 장식 요구 사항이 있습니까
② 음식에 대한 특별한 선호 사항이 있습니까
④ 염두에 둔 특정 분위기가 있습니까

어휘 assist 돕다 event 행사 organize 준비하다 graduation 졸업
expect 예상하다 budget 예산 in mind 염두에 둔
look to ~할 예정이다 aim 목표로 하다 preferably 가급적이면
venue 장소 tailored to ~에 맞춘 preference 선호
requirement 요구 사항 atmosphere 분위기

정답 ③

068 밑줄 친 부분에 들어갈 말로 가장 적절한 것은?

> A: 최근에 뉴스는 계속 보고 있어?
> B: 응, 다소 정신이 없어. 세상에는 너무 많은 일이 일어나고 있어.
> A: 나도 알아. 때때로 따라가기 어렵지. 관심이 가는 뉴스 제목은 뭐가 있어?
> B: 새로운 환경 정책들이 가망 있는 것 같아. 우리가 행동에 나설 때야.
> A: 물론이지. 그것들이 변화를 가져오길 바라.

① 북극곰에 관한 그 뉴스 봤어?
② 환경 운동에 참여한 적 있어?
③ 체벌에 대한 네 생각은 뭐야?

어휘 hectic 정신없는 keep up 따라가다 promising 가망이 있는
It's about time ~할 때이다 take action 행동에 옮기다
make a difference 변화를 가져오다 short 짧은 영상
corporal punishment 체벌 attention 관심

정답 ④

DAY 07   63

069 밑줄 친 부분에 들어갈 말로 가장 적절한 것은?

Austin Blake: Hey! The weather lately has been amazing. I really want to go camping! 10:42

Carrie Bradshaw: Hi! Yeah, I've been itching to go camping too. 10:43

Austin Blake: If we go to the mountains, we can do some trekking, or go to a river for fishing! 10:44

Carrie Bradshaw: That sounds perfect! And we can also make a campfire at night. 10:45

Austin Blake: _____? 10:46

Carrie Bradshaw: A weekend would be ideal for everyone to go camping. How about next weekend? 10:47

Austin Blake: Sounds good! Let's go next weekend then. I'm really looking forward to it! 10:48

Carrie Bradshaw: Yes, me too! 10:49

① When would be a good time
② When have you been camping before
③ What's your favorite activity to do while camping
④ When would you like to make camping plan

070 밑줄 친 부분에 들어갈 말로 가장 적절한 것은?

When we both started working from home permanently, we argued and got _____ with each other all the time.

① soothed   ② concerned
③ pleased   ④ irritated

069 밑줄 친 부분에 들어갈 말로 가장 적절한 것은?

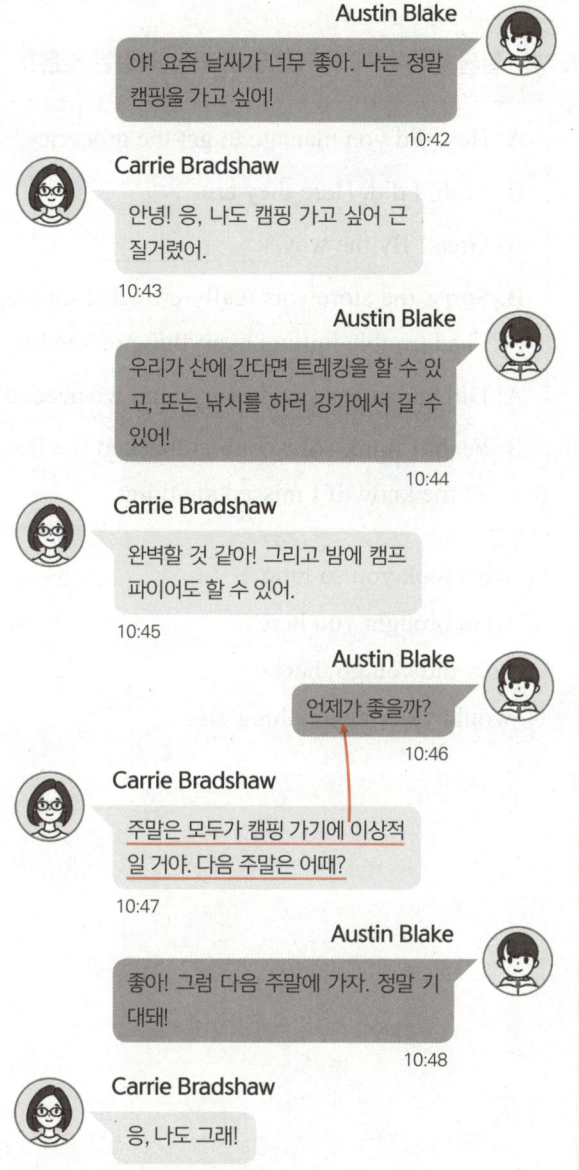

② 전에 언제 캠핑을 가봤어
③ 캠핑할 때 가장 좋아하는 활동이 뭐야
④ 언제 캠핑 계획을 세우고 싶어

어휘 **lately** 요즘 **amazing** 너무 좋은 **itch** (몹시 ~하고 싶어) 근질거리다
trekking 트레킹: 산이나 계곡 따위를 다니는 도보 여행
ideal 이상적인

정답 ①

070

해석 우리 둘 다 영구적으로 재택근무를 시작했을 때, 우리는 항상 서로 다투고 화가 났다.

어휘 **work from home** 재택근무를 하다 **permanently** 영구적으로
argue 다투다 **soothe** 달래다 **concern** 걱정하게 하다
please 기쁘게 하다 **irritate** 화나게 하다

근거

> When we both started working from home permanently, we argued and got irritated with each other all the time.

정답 ④

주요 어휘 정리

irritated 몹시 화가 난	soothe 완화시키다
= furious	= relax
indignant	relieve
infuriated	alleviate
enraged	calm

071 밑줄 친 부분에 들어갈 말로 가장 적절한 것은?

> She is trying to be _____ to avoid a racial prejudice.

① picky ② political
③ impartial ④ biased

072 밑줄 친 부분에 들어갈 말로 가장 적절한 것은?

> Journalism is a notoriously _____ profession. Downsizing and layoffs are almost routine, and many journalists find themselves bouncing between news organizations and periods of freelance work during their careers.

① pecuniary ② conventional
③ prolonged ④ precarious

073 밑줄 친 부분에 들어갈 말로 가장 적절한 것은?

> A: Hey, did you manage to get the groceries?
> B: Yeah, I did. Here they are.
> A: Great! By the way, _____?
> B: Sorry, the store was really crowded today, and I had trouble finding everything on the list.
> A: Did you at least find everything we needed?
> B: Yeah, I think so. I double-checked the list, but let me know if I missed anything.

① what took you so long
② what brought you here
③ how did you go there
④ would you like anything else

071

해석 그녀는 인종적 편견을 피하기 위해 공정하려고 노력하고 있다.

어휘 avoid 피하다   racial 인종적인   prejudice 편견   picky 까다로운
political 정치의   impartial 공정한   biased 편향된

근거

> She is trying to be impartial to avoid a racial prejudice.

정답 ③

주요 어휘 정리
impartial 공정한
= fair
  just
  unbiased
  equitable

072

해석 언론계는 악명 높게 불안정한 직업이다. 인원 감축과 정리 해고는 거의 일상적이고, 많은 기자들은 자신의 경력 동안에 언론사와 프리랜스 작업 기간 사이를 움직이는 스스로를 발견한다.

어휘 journalism 언론계   notoriously 악명 높게
profession 직업, 업계   downsizing 인원 감축   layoff 정리 해고
routine 일상적인   pecuniary 금전상의   conventional 관습적인
prolonged 오래 계속되는, 장기적인   precarious 불안정한

근거

> Journalism is a notoriously precarious profession. Downsizing and layoffs are almost routine, and many journalists find themselves bouncing between news organizations and periods of freelance work during their careers.

정답 ④

주요 어휘 정리
pecuniary 금전상의   precarious 불안정한
= monetary   = insecure
  financial   unstable

073 밑줄 친 부분에 들어갈 말로 가장 적절한 것은?

> A: 저기, 식료품은 어떻게든 구한거야?
> B: 응, 구했지. 여기 있어.
> A: 좋아! 그건 그렇고, 왜 이렇게 오래 걸렸어?
> B: 미안해, 오늘 매장이 정말 붐볐고, 목록에 있는 걸 전부 찾는 데 어려움을 겪었어.
> A: 우리가 필요한 건 최소한 다 찾았니?
> B: 응, 그런 것 같아. 목록을 다시 확인했는데 누락한 거 있으면 말해줘.

② 여긴 어쩐 일이야
③ 거기에 어떻게 갔어
④ 더 필요한 거 없어

어휘 manage (어떻게든) 하다   grocery 식료품
have trouble -ing ~하는 데 어려움을 겪다   at least 적어도
double-check 다시 확인하다   by the way 그건 그렇고
What took you so long? 왜 이렇게 오래 걸렸니?
What brought you here? 여긴 어쩐 일이야?

정답 ①

DAY 08   67

074 밑줄 친 부분에 들어갈 말로 가장 적절한 것은?

A: I see you're preparing for the client presentation. Do you need any help with the final details?
B: Thanks for asking, but I'm all set. I reviewed everything this morning.
A: Great to hear! Then, _____?
B: What? The last time I checked, it was the Grace Hall.
A: Well, it will be held in the Purcell Room. The final decision was made at the meeting this morning.
B: Phew, I would be in big trouble if you didn't mention it.

① didn't we all agreed on the plan without debate
② do you know the venue of the event has changed
③ did you hear the Purcell Room is under repair
④ will you let me know if there are any further updates

075 밑줄 친 부분에 들어갈 말로 가장 적절한 것은?

The final proposal to meet the original objection to radical changes claims that alterations will be made through a _____ process, not all at once.

① extensive   ② limited
③ rapid   ④ gradual

076 밑줄 친 부분에 들어갈 말로 가장 적절한 것은?

Often, if not always, in the first half of a film a lot of new dynamic ideas and plots are introduced, only to be _____ and compromised in the second half.

① indifferent   ② belligerent
③ diluted   ④ contentious

074 밑줄 친 부분에 들어갈 말로 가장 적절한 것은?

> A: 고객 설명회 준비 중이시군요. 최종 세부 사항에 대해 도움이 필요하신가요?
> B: 물어봐 줘서 고맙지만, 전 준비가 다 됐어요. 오늘 아침에 다 검토하고 최종적으로 조정했거든요.
> A: 다행이네요! 그러면, 행사 장소가 변경되었다는 건 알고 있어요?
> B: 네? 제 기억으로는, Grace Hall이었는데요.
> A: 음, 행사는 Purcell Room에서 열릴 거예요. 오늘 아침 회의에서 최종 결정이 났어요.
> B: 휴, 당신이 말해주지 않았으면 전 큰 곤경에 처할 뻔했어요.

① 우리 모두 논쟁 없이 계획에 찬성하지 않았나요
③ Purcell Room이 수리 중이라는 거 알고 있어요
④ 어떤 추가 변경 정보라도 생기면 알려주시겠어요

어휘 all set 준비가 된 the last time I checked 내 기억으로는
mention 말하다 venue 장소 under repair 수리 중인

정답 ②

075

해석 급진적인 변화에 대한 최초의 반대를 충족하는 최종 계획은 변경이 한꺼번에 아니라 점진적인 과정을 통해 이루어질 것이라고 주장한다.

어휘 proposal 계획 objection 반대 radical 급진적인
claim 주장하다 alteration 변화 process 과정
all at once 한꺼번에 extensive 광범위한 limited 제한적인
rapid 빠른 gradual 점진적인

근거

> The final proposal to meet the original objection to radical changes claims that alterations will be made through a gradual process, not all at once.

정답 ④

주요 어휘 정리
gradual 점진적인, 서서히 하는
= moderate
  unhurried
  progressive
  steady
  slow

076

해석 항상 그렇지는 않더라도, 종종 영화의 전반부에서는 많은 새로운 역동적인 아이디어와 줄거리가 소개되지만, 후반부에는 약화되고 절충될 뿐이다.

어휘 first half 전반부 film 영화 compromise 절충하다
second half 후반부 indifferent 무관심한 belligerent 적대적인
dilute 약화시키다, 묽어지다 contentious 논쟁을 좋아하는

근거

> Often, if not always, in the first half of a film a lot of new dynamic ideas and plots are introduced, only to be diluted and compromised in the second half.

정답 ③

주요 어휘 정리
callous 무관심한, 냉담한   belligerent 적대적인, 호전적인
= indifferent   = warlike
  uninterested   aggressive
  disinterested   antagonistic
  apathetic   hostile
  aloof   bellicose
  nonchalant   inimical

077 밑줄 친 부분에 들어갈 말로 가장 적절한 것은?

A: Do you have any plan for this weekend?
B: I'm thinking about bringing my kids to the Lake Park.
A: _____
B: What for? As far as I know it was in fairly good shape.
A: It will be converted into a parking lot.
B: No way! Kids need a safe place to play.

① But the Park is under construction.
② Why don't we go to the Park together?
③ I need to find a place to park my car.
④ Have you ever been to the Park before?

078 밑줄 친 부분에 들어갈 말로 가장 적절한 것은?

A: Oh no! I have a loose tooth.
B: Seriously? You should go see a dentist before it's too late.
A: No. I will just leave it as it is.
B: However, _____
A: Yeah, it could. Delaying it doesn't make it any easier.
B: Good call! The sooner begun, the sooner done.

① it takes courage to see a dentist.
② how about taking it easy?
③ allow time to get over the illness.
④ what if it get worse than that?

077 밑줄 친 부분에 들어갈 말로 가장 적절한 것은?

> A: 이번 주말에 무슨 계획이라도 있어?
> B: 아이들을 호수 공원에 데려갈지 생각 중이야.
> A: 하지만 그 공원은 공사 중인데.
> B: 무엇 때문에? 내가 알기로 공원은 상태가 꽤 좋았는데.
> A: 공원이 주차장으로 바뀐대.
> B: 절대 안 돼! 아이들은 놀 수 있는 안전한 장소가 필요해.

② 그 공원에 같이 갈래?
③ 내 차를 주차할 장소를 찾아야 해.
④ 예전에 그 공원에 가본 적이 있어?

어휘 as far as I know 내가 알기로 in good shape 상태가 좋은
convert 바꾸다   under construction 공사 중인

정답 ①

---

078 밑줄 친 부분에 들어갈 말로 가장 적절한 것은?

> A: 어머! 나 이가 흔들려.
> B: 진짜? 너무 늦기 전에 치과에 가야 해.
> A: 아니야. 그냥 이대로 둘래.
> B: 하지만, 그보다 더 나빠지면 어떻게 해?
> A: 그래, 그럴 수도 있겠다. 그걸 미룬다고 그게 더 쉬워지는 건 아니니까.
> B: 좋은 결정이야! 매도 먼저 맞는 게 나아.

① 치과에 가는 건 용기가 필요해.
② 마음을 편히 먹는 게 어때?
③ 질병에서 회복할 시간을 줘.

어휘 delay 미루다   good call 좋은 결정
The sooner begun, the sooner done. 매도 먼저 맞는 게 낫다.
courage 용기   painkiller 진통제   take it easy 마음을 편히 먹다
get over ~에서 회복하다   illness 질병

정답 ④

079 밑줄 친 부분에 들어갈 말로 가장 적절한 것은?

Rena Bradley: Hey Mark, how's it going? 10:42

Mark Spencer: I'm thinking about new career opportunities. Feeling stuck in my current job. 10:43

Rena Bradley: I get it. Did you start looking into other jobs? 10:44

Mark Spencer: Yeah, I browsed and updated my resume, but it's overwhelming. 10:45

Rena Bradley: Change can be daunting, but it's necessary for growth. _____? 10:46

Mark Spencer: I'm looking for growth in project management. 10:47

Rena Bradley: Good choice. I'm sure you'll find the right fit soon. 10:48

Mark Spencer: Thanks, I will keep you posted. 10:49

① What kind of role are you interested in
② Have you applied to any companies recently
③ Are you reaching out to your contacts for help
④ Why are you considering a job change

080 밑줄 친 부분에 들어갈 말로 가장 적절한 것은?

When falling short of chairs, they can't ask guests to offer their seats to others, so such sacrifice should be _____; it's not an obligation.

① voluntary ② coercive
③ mandatory ④ instinctive

079 밑줄 친 부분에 들어갈 말로 가장 적절한 것은?

② 최근에 지원한 회사가 있니
③ 도움을 요청하기 위해 인맥들에게 연락하고 있니
④ 이직을 고려하는 이유는 무엇이니

어휘 stuck 갇힌 I get it. 알 거 같아. look into ~을 알아보다
browse 훑어보다 resume 이력서
overwhelming 엄두가 안 나는 daunting 힘든
necessary 필요한 management 관리 right fit 딱 맞는 것
keep someone posted (최신 진행 상황을) 계속 알리다
apply 지원하다 reach out 연락하다 contact 연줄(이 닿는 사람)
job change 이직

정답 ①

080

해석 의자가 부족할 때, 그들이 손님에게 의자를 다른 사람에게 양보하라고 요구할 수 없으므로, 그런 희생은 자발적이어야 한다: 그것은 의무가 아니다.

어휘 fall short of ~이 부족하다 sacrifice 희생 obligation 의무
voluntary 자발적인 coercive 강압적인 mandatory 의무적인
instinctive 본능적인

근거
> When falling short of chairs, they can't ask guests to offer their seats to others, so such sacrifice should be voluntary; it's not an obligation.

정답 ①

주요 어휘 정리

run out of ~을 다 써버리다
= use up
  eat up
  exhaust
  deplete

put up with ~을 참다, 참고 견디다
= endure
  tolerate
  stand
  bear

mandatory 의무적인
= compulsory
  obligatory
  required

081 밑줄 친 부분에 들어갈 말로 가장 적절한 것은?

> Most Americans were _____ with the Cubans, viewing their struggle for independence with empathy, but President Cleveland was determined to preserve neutrality.

① unfeeling ② indifferent
③ unfriendly ④ sympathetic

082 밑줄 친 부분에 들어갈 말로 가장 적절한 것은?

> Despite the economic upheaval of a global pandemic, generous donors showed their _____ for people in need around the world.

① compassion ② profitability
③ contradiction ④ severance

083 밑줄 친 부분에 들어갈 말로 가장 적절한 것은?

> A doctor who _____ confidential information about patients is not behaving professionally. Doctors have to protect patients' personal information from improper disclosure.

① reveals ② conceals
③ reflects ④ alters

081

해석 대부분의 미국인은 쿠바인에게 동정적이었고, 그들의 독립을 위한 투쟁을 공감하며 보았지만, 클리블랜드 대통령은 중립을 지키기로 결심했다.

어휘 Cuban 쿠바인 struggle 투쟁 independence 독립
president 대통령 be determined to ~하기로 결심하다
preserve 지키다 neutrality 중립 empathy 공감
unfeeling 냉정한 indifferent 무관심한 unfriendly 불친절한
sympathetic 동정적인

근거

> Most Americans were sympathetic with the Cubans, viewing their struggle for independence with empathy, but President Cleveland was determined to preserve neutrality.

정답 ④

주요 어휘 정리
sympathetic 동정적인
= pitiful
  compassionate

082

해석 세계적인 유행병의 경제적 격변에도 불구하고, 후한 기부자들은 전 세계의 도움이 필요한 사람들에 대한 그들의 연민을 보여줬다.

어휘 upheaval 격변 pandemic 세계적 유행병
generous 후한 donor 기부자 compassion 연민
profitability 수익성 contradiction 모순 severance 단절

근거

> Despite the economic upheaval of a global pandemic, generous donors showed their compassion for people in need around the world.

정답 ①

주요 어휘 정리
upheaval 격변, 소란	compassion 연민, 동정심
= chaos	= sympathy
tumult	mercy
turmoil	pity
confusion	kindness
uproar	

083

해석 환자에 대한 기밀을 누설하는 의사는 전문가답게 행동하는 것이 아니다. 의사들은 환자의 개인 정보를 부적절한 공개로부터 보호해야 한다.

어휘 confidential 기밀의 patient 환자
personal information 개인 정보 improper 부적절한
disclosure 공개 reveal 누설하다 conceal 감추다
reflect 반영하다 alter 변경하다

근거

> A doctor who reveals confidential information about patients is not behaving professionally. Doctors have to protect patients' personal information from improper disclosure.

정답 ①

주요 어휘 정리
reveal 누설하다, 드러내다	alter 바꾸다
= disclose	= change
debunk	adjust
divulge	amend
unveil	modify
uncover	revise
unearth	rectify
let on	

084 밑줄 친 부분에 들어갈 말로 가장 적절한 것은?

> He was greeted with the warm and _____ welcome when his name was read out.

① passive ② hospitable
③ hostile   ④ confidential

085 밑줄 친 부분에 들어갈 말로 가장 적절한 것은?

> These domestic skills are _____ from mother to daughter, through the generations. Often the lessons are learned by chance — as a daughter plays in the room while a mother sews or cooks.

① regressed ② eradicated
③ converted ④ inherited

086 밑줄 친 부분에 들어갈 말로 가장 적절한 것은?

 Harper Beckham
These days, I'm really struggling because I don't have enough money.
10:42

 Ember Leigh
I hear you. Money issues can be really stressful. But managing your budget can definitely help improve things.
10:43

 **Harper Beckham**
_____
10:44

 Ember Leigh
First, try organizing your income and expenses each month.
10:45

 Harper Beckham
Yeah, that sounds like a good idea. That'll let me know where my money goes and where I can cut back.
10:46

 Ember Leigh
It might be challenging at first, but once it becomes a habit, it'll really pay off.
10:47

 Harper Beckham
Thanks, buddy.
10:48

① What should I write in my planner?
② Why don't you learn about accounting?
③ How should I go about managing my money?
④ How could I organize my database?

084

해석 그의 이름이 불렸을 때 그는 따뜻하고 친절한 환영을 받았다.

어휘 greet 환영하다　read out 부르다　passive 수동적인
hospitable 친절한　hostile 호전적인　confidential 비밀의

근거

> He was greeted with the warm and hospitable welcome when his name was read out.

정답 ②

주요 어휘 정리

hospitable 친절한, 환대하는
= welcoming　friendly
　agreeable　congenial
　affable　genial
　amiable　cordial
　amicable

hostile 호전적인, 적대적인
= warlike　belligerent
　antagonistic　bellicose
　aggressive　inimical

085

해석 이러한 가정 기술은 어머니에서 딸로 세대를 통해 물려 받아진다. 어머니가 바느질을 하거나 요리를 하는 동안 딸이 방에서 놀면서 교육은 종종 우연히 일어난다.

어휘 domestic 가정의　generation 세대　by chance 우연히
sew 바느질하다　regress 퇴보하다　eradicate 근절하다
convert 전환하다　inherit 물려받다

근거

> These domestic skills are inherited from mother to daughter, through the generations. Often the lessons are learned by chance — as a daughter plays in the room while a mother sews or cooks.

정답 ④

주요 어휘 정리

preserve 보존하다, 보호하다
= conserve
　maintain
　protect
　sustain
　shield
　safeguard

eradicate 근절하다, 뿌리째 뽑다
= remove
　eliminate
　exterminate
　get rid of
　wipe out
　sweep out
　weed out
　root out

086 밑줄 친 부분에 들어갈 말로 가장 적절한 것은?

 Harper Beckham
요즘, 나는 돈이 충분하지 않아서 정말 허우적거리고 있어.
10:42

 Ember Leigh
그래 알아 무슨 말인지. 돈 문제는 정말 스트레스가 될 수 있어. 하지만 예산을 관리하는 것이 분명히 상황을 개선하는 데 도움이 될 수 있어.
10:43

 Harper Beckham
내 돈을 어떻게 관리하기 시작해야 할까?
10:44

 Ember Leigh
먼저, 매달 수입과 지출을 정리해 봐.
10:45

 Harper Beckham
그래, 그거 좋은 생각인 것 같아. 네 돈이 어디로 가는지 아는 것이 네가 어디를 줄여야 할지를 알려줄 수 있어.
10:46

 Ember Leigh
처음에는 어려울 수도 있지만, 일단 습관이 되면, 정말 효과가 있을 거야.
10:47

 Harper Beckham
고마워, 친구야.
10:48

① 내 플래너에 뭘 적어야 할까?
② 회계학에 대해 공부하는 게 어때?
④ 내 자료를 어떻게 정리할 수 있을까?

어휘 struggle 허우적대다　I hear you. 그래 알아 무슨 말인지.
stressful 스트레스가 되는　manage 관리하다　budget 예산
definitely 분명히　organize 정리하다　income 수입
expense 지출　cut back 줄이다　challenging 어려운
pay off 효과가 있다　buddy 친구　accounting 회계학
go about 시작하다

정답 ③

087 밑줄 친 부분에 들어갈 말로 가장 적절한 것은?

> A: I'm in 507. I have a problem with my room.
> B: What is the problem, sir?
> A: There are cockroaches in my room.
> B: Are you sure, sir? Flies, I could believe, but cockroaches?
> A: I've counted nine different cockroaches, and I accidentally stepped on another one.
> B: Sir, _____.
> A: You dare to doubt me?
> B: I'm sorry, sir. Let me transfer you to my supervisor.

① we tried in vain to address the cockroach problem
② you are not eligible to flatter yourself in this case
③ I'm sorry that your room is not made up and ready
④ this hotel passed a thorough insect inspection perfectly

088 밑줄 친 부분에 들어갈 말로 가장 적절한 것은?

Emma Thomson: Hey, do you have any vacation plans coming up? 10:42

Jake Miller: Hi Emma! Yes, I'm planning a trip to Hawaii next month. How about you? 10:43

Emma Thomson: I'm thinking of going to Italy later this year. Any specific places you're excited to visit in Hawaii? 10:44

Jake Miller: Definitely! The beaches in Maui and Volcanoes National Park. _____? 10:45

Emma Thomson: Exploring Rome and visiting the Colosseum, and of course, the food. 10:46

Jake Miller: Have a fantastic trip! 10:47

Emma Thomson: Thanks! You too. Let's share stories when we're back. 10:48

① What are you looking forward to in Italy
② What's the best accommodation you've stayed in
③ Do you have any travel tips for staying safe abroad
④ How do you manage your budget while traveling

087 밑줄 친 부분에 들어갈 말로 가장 적절한 것은?

> A: 507호입니다. 제 방에 문제가 있어요.
> B: 무슨 문제죠, 선생님?
> A: 제 방에 바퀴벌레가 있어요.
> B: 확실하세요? 파리라면 믿겠지만, 바퀴벌레요?
> A: 제가 아홉 마리의 바퀴벌레를 셌고, 뜻하지 않게 다른 바퀴벌레를 밟았어요.
> B: 선생님, 이 호텔은 철저한 벌레 검사를 완벽하게 통과했습니다.
> A: 감히 나를 의심하는 건가요?
> B: 죄송합니다, 선생님. 관리자에게 연결해드리겠습니다.

① 저희는 바퀴벌레 문제를 해결하려고 노력했지만 허사였습니다
② 당신은 이 상황에서는 자만할 자격이 없습니다
③ 당신의 방이 준비되지 않은 것에 대해 죄송합니다

어휘 cockroach 바퀴벌레　fly 파리　accidentally 뜻하지 않게
doubt 의심하다　in vain 허사가 되어　address 해결하다
eligible 자격이 있는　flatter oneself 자만하다
make up 준비하다　thorough 철저한　inspection 검사

정답 ④

088 밑줄 친 부분에 들어갈 말로 가장 적절한 것은?

② 당신이 묵었던 최고의 숙소는 어디야
③ 해외에서 안전하게 지낼 수 있는 여행 팁이 있니
④ 여행 중에 예산을 어떻게 관리하니

어휘 vacation 휴가　come up 다가오다　specific 구체적인
definitely 물론이지　explore 탐험하다　fantastic 멋진
accommodation 숙소　abroad 해외에서

정답 ①

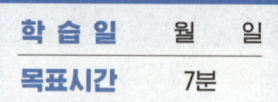

089 밑줄 친 부분에 들어갈 말로 가장 적절한 것은?

A: How long in advance can I book a meeting room for?
B: Meetings may be scheduled up to 4 weeks in advance.
A: Then, I want to schedule a meeting for September 9th.
B: Let me see, oh, that day is fully booked.
A: Oh, no! _____
B: You can sign up for alerts, and you'll get an automated message if a reservation spot opens up.

① Do you think now is as good time as any?
② I have a very tight schedule on that day.
③ Can you notify me if there is an opening?
④ I think I can reschedule it for October 9th.

090 밑줄 친 부분에 들어갈 말로 가장 적절한 것은?

A: Hey, why are you so upset?
B: I heard big news. They're planning to lay off some people next month.
A: Where did you get that information?
B: From a friend in HR. How come you don't seem surprised?
A: _____
B: Really? Oh, my gosh. That kind of groundless gossip makes me worn out.

① I have gone too far with this gossip.
② Because It turned out to be a rumor.
③ I was very upset to hear that statement.
④ I assure you HR is a reliable source.

문장 분석 및 해설

089 밑줄 친 부분에 들어갈 말로 가장 적절한 것은?

> A: 회의실 예약을 얼마나 미리 할 수 있나요?
> B: 회의는 4주까지 미리 예약될 수 있어요.
> A: 그러면, 9월 9일에 회의를 예약하고 싶어요.
> B: 어디 보자, 오, 그날은 예약이 꽉 찼어요.
> A: 아, 안 되는데! 빈자리가 생기면 저에게 알려주시겠어요?
> B: 알림을 신청하면, 예약 자리가 생길 때 자동 메시지를 받을 거예요.

① 지금이 가장 좋은 시기라고 생각하세요?
② 저는 그날 일정이 아주 꽉 찼어요.
④ 10월 9일로 일정을 다시 잡아도 될 것 같아요.

어휘 book 예약하다   in advance 미리   sign up for ~을 신청하다
alert 알림   reservation 예약   automate 자동화하다

정답 ③

090 밑줄 친 부분에 들어갈 말로 가장 적절한 것은?

> A: 이봐, 왜 그렇게 화가 났어?
> B: 엄청난 소식을 들었거든. 다음 달에 몇 명을 해고할 계획이래.
> A: 어디서 그 소식을 얻었어?
> B: 인사부에 있는 친구한테. 어째서 너는 놀란 것처럼 보이지 않는데?
> A: 왜냐하면 그건 헛소문으로 밝혀졌거든.
> B: 정말? 아, 세상에. 그런 종류의 소문은 날 매우 지치게 해.

① 그 소문 가지고 내가 너무 지나쳤어.
③ 그 발표를 듣고 나는 몹시 화가 났어.
④ 인사부가 믿을 만한 소식통인 건 내가 보장해.

어휘 upset 화가 난   how come 어째서   groundless 근거 없는
worn out 매우 지친   statement 발표   assure 보장하다
reliable 믿을 만한

정답 ②

091 밑줄 친 부분에 들어갈 말로 가장 적절한 것은?

> Negotiations between the sides are still underway, but industry observers believe an agreement is _____.

① imminent ② principal
③ solitary ④ innate

092 밑줄 친 부분에 들어갈 말로 가장 적절한 것은?

> French fries and soda might be delicious, but too much of these foods can leave you feeling achy and tired, and can even _____ your health.

① maintain ② improve
③ diagnose ④ worsen

093 밑줄 친 부분에 들어갈 말로 가장 적절한 것은?

> A: I noticed you haven't finished your part yet. The deadline is coming.
> B: Well, you were also late with the last project.
> A: You had multiple delays with many projects.
> B: Fair point, but _____
> A: Yeah, that's true. What really counts is we get this right and on time.
> B: Sure, let's meet the deadline, at least this time.

① we need to decide what is right and wrong.
② I heard the project deadline was pushed back.
③ what good is it to argue about who is at fault?
④ how on earth do they count it as a delay?

091

해석 양측 간의 협상은 아직 진행 중이지만, 업계 관찰자들은 합의가 <u>임박한</u> 것으로 믿고 있다.

어휘 negotiation 협상   underway 진행 중인   industry 업계
observer 관찰자   agreement 합의   imminent 임박한
principal 주된   solitary 혼자 하는   innate 타고난

근거

> Negotiations between the sides are still underway, but industry observers believe an agreement is imminent.

정답 ①

주요 어휘 정리

imminent 임박한	innate 타고난
= urgent	= inborn
emergent	inherent
pressing	hereditary
imperative	natural
impending	

092

해석 감자튀김과 탄산음료는 맛이 있을지는 모르지만, 너무 많은 이런 음식은 당신을 아프고 피곤하며, 심지어 당신의 건강을 <u>악화시킬</u> 수 있다.

어휘 achy 아픈   tired 피곤한   maintain 유지하다   improve 개선하다
diagnose 진단하다   worsen 악화시키다

근거

> French fries and soda might be delicious, but too much of these foods can leave you feeling achy and tired, and can even worsen your health.

정답 ④

주요 어휘 정리

improve 개선하다	worsen 악화시키다 / 악화되다	
= ameliorate	= aggravate	= deteriorate
reform	exacerbate	degenerate

093 밑줄 친 부분에 들어갈 말로 가장 적절한 것은?

> A: 네가 맡은 부분을 아직 끝내지 못한 걸로 알고 있어. 마감일이 다가오고 있다고.
> B: 글쎄, 지난 프로젝트 때는 너도 늦었잖아.
> A: 너는 여러 프로젝트에서 여러 번 지연시켰잖아.
> B: 타당한 지적이긴 한데, <u>누가 잘못했는지를 따지는 게 무슨 소용이야?</u>
> A: 그래, 맞는 말이야. 정말로 중요한 건 우리가 이 일을 제대로 제때 하는 거야.
> B: 맞아, 적어도 이번에는 마감일을 맞춰보자.

① 뭐가 옳고 뭐가 그른지 결정할 필요가 있어.
② 프로젝트 마감일이 뒤로 미뤄졌다고 들었어.
④ 도대체 어떻게 그걸 지연에 포함시킬 수 있어?

어휘 deadline 마감일   multiple 다수의   delay 지연
count 중요하다, 포함시키다   push back ~을 뒤로 미루다
at fault 잘못인   on earth 도대체

정답 ③

DAY 10

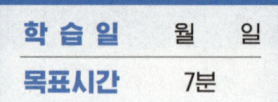

094 밑줄 친 부분에 들어갈 말로 가장 적절한 것은?

> A: Hey, I'm moving into my new apartment tomorrow. Could you lend me a hand with moving stuff?
> B: Sure thing! What are neighbors for?
> A: Thanks a lot! Can you come over here around noon?
> B: No problem. Should I bring any tools or just my muscles?
> A: _____.
> B: I see. I'll bring my tool box with me.

① Buy tools in a nearby store
② Movers will take care of it
③ Just your muscles should do
④ I need to drive some screws

095 밑줄 친 부분에 들어갈 말로 가장 적절한 것은?

> Journalists must be _____. For instance, they must be good at writing, listening to people, speaking, working quickly, and doing research.

① fastidious   ② contemporary
③ extensive   ④ versatile

096 밑줄 친 부분에 들어갈 말로 가장 적절한 것은?

> When faced with a shortage of funds, the company had to _____ to borrowing from investors to continue its operations.

① resort   ② cater
③ object   ④ react

094 밑줄 친 부분에 들어갈 말로 가장 적절한 것은?

> A: 안녕, 나 내일 새 아파트로 이사 가. 짐 옮기는 것 좀 도와줄 수 있어?
> B: 물론이지! 이웃 좋다는 게 뭐야?
> A: 정말 고마워! 정오쯤에 건너와 줄래?
> B: 그럼. 도구를 가져갈까 아니면 그냥 몸만 갈까?
> A: 나사못을 몇 군데 박아야 할 것 같아.
> B: 알겠어. 내 공구 상자를 가져갈게.

① 근처 가게에서 공구를 구입해
② 이사꾼들이 해결할 거야
③ 그냥 몸만 와도 충분해

어휘 lend a hand 도와주다　sure thing 물론
What are neighbors for? 이웃 좋다는 게 뭐야?　nearby 근처의
do 되다[충분하다]

정답 ④

095

해석 기자는 다재다능해야 한다. 예를 들어, 그들은 글을 쓰는 것, 사람들의 말을 듣는 것, 말하는 것, 신속히 일하는 것, 조사를 하는 것에 능숙해야 한다.

어휘 journalist 기자　be good at ~에 능숙하다　fastidious 꼼꼼한
contemporary 동시대의, 현대의　extensive 아주 넓은, 광범위한
versatile 다재다능한

근거

> Journalists must be versatile. For instance, they must be good at writing, listening to people, speaking, working quickly, and doing research.

정답 ④

주요 어휘 정리

fastidious 꼼꼼한, 세심한	versatile 다재다능한
= meticulous	= well-rounded
scrupulous	all-around
punctilious	all-purpose
careful	
thorough	

096

해석 자금 부족에 직면했을 때, 그 회사는 회사의 운영을 위해 투자자들로부터 빌리는데 의지해야 했다.

어휘 shortage 부족　fund 자금　borrow 빌리다　investor 투자자
operation 운영　resort 의지하다　cater 음식을 공급하다
object 반대하다　react 반응하다

근거

> When faced with a shortage of funds, the company had to resort to borrowing from investors to continue its operations.

정답 ①

097 밑줄 친 부분에 들어갈 말로 가장 적절한 것은?

> A: My throat is really dry.
> B: Do you want to go get something to drink?
> A: Let's do that.
> B: What did you want to drink?
> A: I was thinking about getting some soda.
> B: _____.
> A: What else should I drink then?
> B: Water is what's best for you.
> A: I guess I will get water.

① Just wait here and I'll just get you a soda
② Oh, no! This vending machine is out of order now
③ You shouldn't drink soda when you're really thirsty
④ A soda is so freshing on a hot day

098 밑줄 친 부분에 들어갈 말로 가장 적절한 것은?

> A: The current timeline is just too tight. I really need an extension on this deadline.
> B: Haven't we already extended the deadline once?
> A: Please, have a heart. I'm dealing with unexpected issues.
> B: The thing is if we delay this any longer, the next project will be delayed as well.
> A: You're right. _____.
> B: That's what I'm talking about! Let's turn over a new leaf.

① We can't keep pushing it back forever
② I need to ensure the quality of the work
③ It's impossible to push the deadline forward
④ I'll have it done by the new deadline

097 밑줄 친 부분에 들어갈 말로 가장 적절한 것은?

> A: 나 목이 너무 말라.
> B: 뭐 좀 마시러 갈래?
> A: 그러자.
> B: 뭐 마시고 싶었어?
> A: 나는 탄산음료를 마실까 생각 중이었어.
> B: 너는 진짜 목마를 때 탄산음료는 마시지 말아야 해.
> A: 그럼 다른 어떤 걸 마셔야 해?
> B: 물이 너한테 가장 좋아.
> A: 물을 마셔야겠다.

① 여기서 기다리면 내가 탄산음료를 가져다줄게
② 안 돼! 이 자판기 지금 고장 났어
④ 탄산음료는 더운 날 정말 상쾌하지

어휘 vending machine 자판기   out of order 고장 난

정답 ③

098 밑줄 친 부분에 들어갈 말로 가장 적절한 것은?

> A: 현재 일정이 너무 빠듯해. 이번 마감일은 정말 연장이 필요해.
> B: 우리가 마감일을 이미 한 번 연장하지 않았어?
> A: 제발, 마음을 써줘. 예상치 못한 문제들을 처리하는 중이란 말이야.
> B: 문제는 우리가 이번 일을 조금이라도 더 미루면, 다음 프로젝트도 미뤄진다는 거야.
> A: 네 말이 맞아. 마감일을 영원히 미룰 수는 없지.
> B: 내 말이 그 말이야! 우리 심기일전하자.

② 나는 작업의 질을 보장해야 해
③ 마감일을 당기는 건 불가능해
④ 새 마감일까지는 일을 끝내게

어휘 current 현재의   tight 빠듯한   extension 연장
have a heart 마음을 쓰다
That's what I'm talking about. 내 말이 그 말이야.
turn over a new leaf 심기일전하다   push back ~을 뒤로 미루다
ensure 보장하다   push forward ~을 앞으로 당기다

정답 ①

099 밑줄 친 부분에 들어갈 말로 가장 적절한 것은?

Anna Denver: Hey Mark, have you seen any good movies lately? 10:42

Mark Strong: Hi Anna! Yes, I watched "Dune" recently. It was visually stunning! How about you? 10:43

Anna Denver: I haven't seen "Dune" yet, but I heard it's amazing. I watched "No Time to Die" last week. Have you seen it? 10:44

Mark Strong: Yes, "No Time to Die" was fantastic! Daniel Craig really nailed it in his final Bond film. What did you think? 10:45

Anna Denver: _____. 10:46

Mark Strong: I agree with you. Well, let's catch up soon and maybe watch a movie together! 10:47

Anna Denver: Sounds like a plan! 10:48

① I struggled to stay awake through the entire film
② I definitely want to see it too because I heard it is really awesome
③ It was so boring that I found myself dozing off during the screening
④ The action scenes were thrilling, and the storyline kept me hooked throughout

100 밑줄 친 부분에 들어갈 말로 가장 적절한 것은?

This surge in travel has created _____ and unforeseen strains on all aspects of the global aviation system.

① unprecedented ② verbose
③ plausible ④ superficial

099 밑줄 친 부분에 들어갈 말로 가장 적절한 것은?

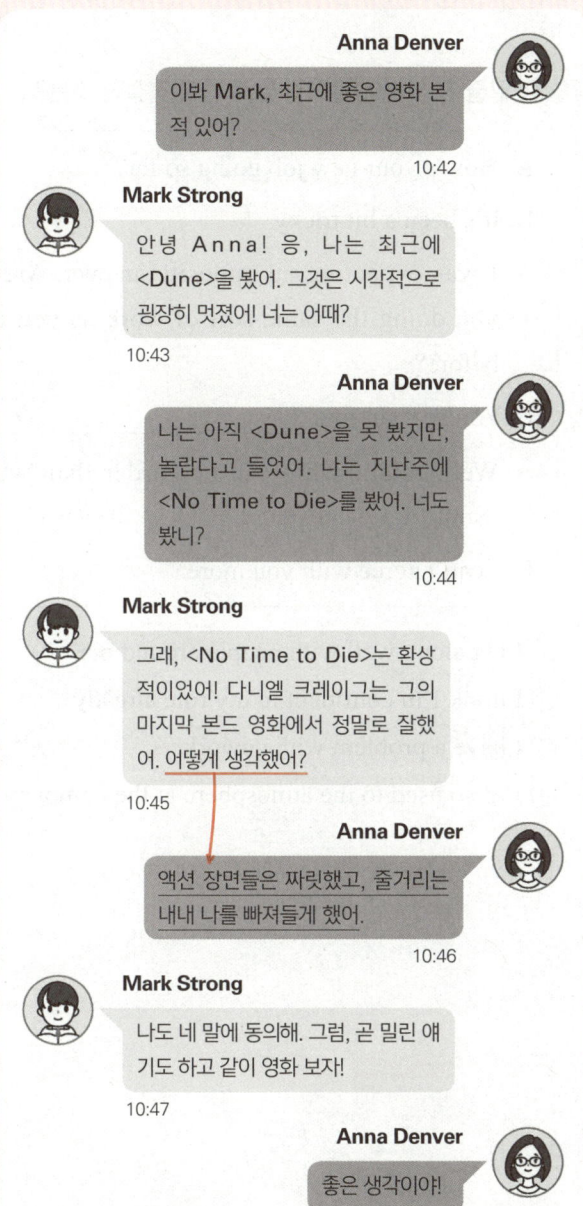

① 나는 영화 내내 깨어 있으려고 애썼어
② 정말 멋지다고 해서 나도 꼭 보고 싶어
③ 너무 지루해서 상영 중에 졸았어

어휘 lately 최근에 recently 최근에 visually 시각적으로
stunning 굉장히 멋진 nail it 정말 잘하다
catch up 밀린 얘기를 하다 struggle 애쓰다 definitely 꼭
awesome 멋진 doze off 졸다 screening (영화) 상영
thrilling 짜릿한 storyline 줄거리 kept me hooked 빠져든
throughout 내내

정답 ④

100

해석 여행의 급증은 전 세계 항공 시스템의 모든 면에 전례 없는 뜻밖의 부담을 만들었다.

어휘 surge 급증 unforeseen 뜻밖의 strain 부담 aviation 항공
unrealizable 실현할 수 없는 unprecedented 전례 없는, 유례없는
verbose 장황한 plausible 그럴듯한
superficial 피상적인, 표면적인

근거

> This surge in travel has created <u>unprecedented</u> and <u>unforeseen</u> strains on all aspects of the global aviation system.

정답 ①

주요 어휘 정리

unprecedented 전례 없는, 유례없는
= unsurpassed
  unheard of
  unaccustomed

verbose 장황한
= talkative
  garrulous
  loquacious
  wordy

superficial 피상적인, 얕은
= shallow

101 밑줄 친 부분에 들어갈 말로 가장 적절한 것은?

> The organization will launch numerous projects to _____ forests in these countries. They will be very helpful to protect the soil from being eroded by wind and rain.

① preserve ② destroy
③ prepare   ④ damage

102 밑줄 친 부분에 들어갈 말로 가장 적절한 것은?

> Public usage of public spaces does not always _____ the expectations of society nor necessarily adhere to the laws of a given time.

① care for   ② dispense with
③ conform to   ④ take after

103 밑줄 친 부분에 들어갈 말로 가장 적절한 것은?

> A: How's your new job going so far?
> B: It's been a bit tricky.
> A: I was expecting an opposite answer. Aren't you doing the same sort of work as you did before?
> B: You're right, but _____.
> A: Well, relationship can be harder than work itself.
> B: I can't agree with you more.

① I get along well with people around me
② I think I'm confident in my role already
③ I have a problem with coworkers
④ I'm so used to the atmosphere at the company

문장 분석 및 해설

101

해석 그 단체는 이 국가들의 숲을 보존하기 위한 수많은 프로젝트를 시작할 것이다. 그것들은 바람과 비에 침식되고 있는 토양을 보호하는 데 매우 도움이 될 것이다.

어휘 organization 단체 launch 시작하다 numerous 수많은
protect 보호하다 soil 토양 erode 침식시키다
preserve 보존하다 destroy 파괴하다 prepare 준비하다
damage 피해를 주다

근거

> The organization will launch numerous projects to preserve forests in these countries. They will be very helpful to protect the soil from being eroded by wind and rain.

정답 ①

preserve 보존하다   destroy 파괴하다
= conserve   = demolish
  maintain   ruin
  protect   wreck
  sustain   devastate
  shield
  safeguard

102

해석 공공장소의 공적 사용이 항상 사회의 기대를 따르는 것은 아니며 특정 시대의 법을 반드시 지키는 것도 아니다.

어휘 expectation 기대 adhere to ~을 지키다 care for ~을 돌보다
dispense with ~ 없이 지내다 conform to ~을 따르다
take after ~을 닮다

근거

> Public usage of public spaces does not always conform to the expectations of society nor necessarily adhere to the laws of a given time.

정답 ③

주요 어휘 정리

care for ~을 돌보다   dispense with ~ 없이 지내다
= take care of   = do without
  look after

conform to ~을 따르다, 지키다   take after ~을 닮다
= follow   comply with   = resemble
  obey   abide by   look like
  observe   keep to
                go by

103 밑줄 친 부분에 들어갈 말로 가장 적절한 것은?

> A: 새 직장은 지금까지 어때요?
> B: 좀 까다로워요.
> A: 저는 반대의 대답을 기대하고 있었는데요. 전에 하던 것과 같은 종류의 일을 하시는 거 아니에요?
> B: 그건 그렇지만, 동료들과 문제가 있어요.
> A: 흠, 인간관계가 일 자체보다 더 어려울 수 있죠.
> B: 전적으로 동의해요.

① 저는 주변 사람들과 잘 지내요
② 저는 벌써 새 직무에 자신감이 생기는 거 같아요
④ 저는 회사 분위기에 정말 익숙해요

어휘 so far 지금까지 tricky 까다로운 opposite 반대의
coworker 동료 relationship 인간관계
I can't agree with you more. 전적으로 동의해요.

정답 ③

DAY 11 91

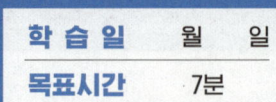

104 밑줄 친 부분에 들어갈 말로 가장 적절한 것은?

_____ people can not only get through hard times but thrive during and after them. Just as a rubber ball rebounds after being squeezed, so do these people.

① Inimical ② Reluctant
③ Susceptible ④ Resilient

105 밑줄 친 부분에 들어갈 말로 가장 적절한 것은?

Both parties have agreed to conclude the negotiations quickly so the bills can be enacted in the current Assembly session. However, even after 10 rounds of negotiations, they have so far failed to _____ an agreement.

① eliminate ② burst
③ withdraw ④ formulate

106 밑줄 친 부분에 들어갈 말로 가장 적절한 것은?

A: I just heard that the company will be rolling out a new performance review system starting next quarter.

B: Really? That's news to me. I haven't seen any announcements about that.

A: Yeah, it was mentioned in a meeting this morning. They said it will affect how we get evaluated and might change some of the criteria.

B: I see. It sounds like a significant change. Do you know when we'll get more details?

A: According to them, _____.

B: Then, I will frequently check out the office bulletin board and my emails.

① as of yet no concrete schedule has been set
② the system reform process went smoothly
③ the bulletin board is used for work related issues
④ they posted the details on the official website

104

해석 회복력 있는 사람들은 힘든 시간을 극복할 수 있을 뿐만 아니라 그 시간 동안 그리고 그 후에도 잘 살 수 있다. 압박을 받은 후 고무공이 다시 튀어 오르듯, 이 사람들도 그렇다.

어휘 get through 극복하다　thrive 잘 살다　rubber ball 고무공　rebound 다시 튀어 오르다　squeeze 압박하다　inimical 적대적인　reluctant 꺼리는

근거

> Resilient people can not only get through hard times but thrive during and after them. Just as a rubber ball rebounds after being squeezed, so do these people.

정답 ④

주요 어휘 정리

susceptible 영향받기 쉬운
= vulnerable

resilient 회복력 있는
= flexible　　plastic
  elastic　　 supple
  pliant　　 adaptable
  pliable

105

해석 양당은 이 법안들이 현 국회 회기에서 제정될 수 있도록 협상을 빨리 끝내기로 합의했다. 그러나 10차례의 협상 이후에도, 그들은 지금까지 합의를 이루는 데 실패했다.

어휘 party 정당　conclude 끝내다　bill 법안　enact 제정하다　assembly 국회　negotiation 협상　so far 지금까지　eliminate 제거하다　burst 터지다　withdraw 철수하다　formulate 만들어 내다

근거

> Both parties have agreed to conclude the negotiations quickly so the bills can be enacted in the current Assembly session. However, even after 10 rounds of negotiations, they have so far failed to formulate an agreement.

정답 ④

주요 어휘 정리

formulate 만들어 내다
= reach
  achieve
  conclude

106 밑줄 친 부분에 들어갈 말로 가장 적절한 것은?

> A: 회사가 다음 분기부터 새로운 성과심사 제도를 시작한다고 방금 들었어요.
> B: 정말요? 저는 금시초문이에요. 저는 그에 대한 발표를 본 적이 없어요.
> A: 네, 오늘 오전에 회의에서 언급한 내용이에요. 그것이 우리가 평가받는 방식에 영향을 미칠 것이고, 기준을 일부 변경할 수도 있다고 했어요.
> B: 그렇군요. 중요한 변화 같네요. 자세한 내용은 언제쯤 받게 될지 아세요?
> A: 회사 측 말로는, 아직 구체적인 일정이 결정되지 않았대요.
> B: 그러면, 사내 게시판과 이메일을 수시로 확인해볼래요.

② 그 제도 개혁 과정은 원활하게 진행되었어요
③ 게시판은 업무 관련 문제 용도로 사용되고 있대요
④ 그들이 자세한 내용을 공식 웹사이트에 공지했대요

어휘 roll out 시작하다　performance 성과　review 심사　quarter 분기　announcement 발표　affect 영향을 미치다　evaluate 평가하다　criterion (pl. criteria) 기준　significant 중요한　frequently 수시로　check out ~을 확인하다　bulletin board 게시판　as of yet 아직　concrete 구체적인　reform 개혁　process 과정　post 게시하다

정답 ①

107 밑줄 친 부분에 들어갈 말로 가장 적절한 것은?

Josh Kang
Hi Naomi, I'm here to give you an update on the project.
10:42

Naomi Brown
Hi Josh, please go ahead.
10:43

Josh Kang
We've received the first draft from the design team. We plan to incorporate the feedback by tomorrow.
10:44

Naomi Brown
Sounds good. _____ _____?
10:45

Josh Kang
The survey data has been collected and analysts is assessing how reliable the sample is.
10:46

Naomi Brown
Got it. Please provide weekly updates on each part's progress.
10:47

Josh Kang
Will do. Thank you.
10:48

① Did you hire analysts under the procedure
② How is marketing research going
③ Can you give a progress report regularly
④ Is there anything I can help you with

108 밑줄 친 부분에 들어갈 말로 가장 적절한 것은?

A: Do you mind if I borrow the notes from last week?
B: Weren't you here last week?
A: I was unable to make it.
B: How come?
A: _____.
B: Oh, you are still looking a bit under the weather. Well, here is my notebook.
A: Yes, thank you so much.
B: It's no problem at all.

① My mom was very ill
② I wasn't feeling well
③ I woke up too late
④ I was counting on you

107 밑줄 친 부분에 들어갈 말로 가장 적절한 것은?

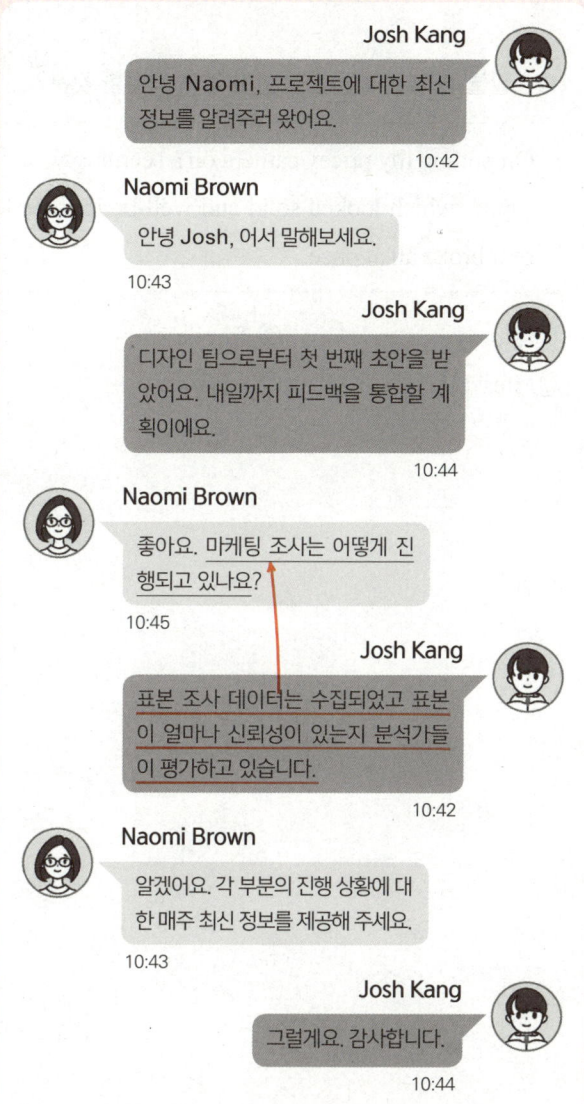

① 분석가들을 절차대로 고용했나요
③ 진행 보고를 정기적으로 해주시겠어요
④ 제가 도와드릴 만한 일이 있을까요

어휘 Go ahead. 어서 해보세요.　draft 초안　incorporate 통합하다
survey 표본 조사　analyst 분석가　assess 평가하다
reliable 신뢰성 있는　sample 표본　hire 채용하다
under the procedure 절차대로　regularly 정기적으로

정답 ②

108 밑줄 친 부분에 들어갈 말로 가장 적절한 것은?

> A: 지난주 필기한 거 빌릴 수 있을까?
> B: 지난주에 여기 없었어?
> A: 나 참석할 수가 없었어.
> B: 어쩌다가?
> A: 몸이 좋지 않았어.
> B: 오, 아직도 조금 아파 보여. 그럼, 내 공책 여기 있어.
> A: 그래, 너무 고마워.
> B: 천만에.

① 엄마가 많이 아프셨어
③ 너무 늦게 일어났어
④ 너를 믿고 있었어

어휘 under the weather 몸이 아픈　count on ~을 믿다

정답 ②

DAY 11　95

109 밑줄 친 부분에 들어갈 말로 가장 적절한 것은?

Ashley Parker
How did the interview with Mr. Roberts go?
10:42

Ben Hogan
I really enjoyed meeting him. He seems smart and organized.
10:43

Ashley Parker
That's great to hear! How did he handled the technical questions?
10:44

Ben Hogan
He handled them really well.
10:45

Ashley Parker
Sounds like he could be a good fit for the team.
10:46

Ben Hogan
Absolutely. He seemed genuinely interested in our company.
10:47

Ashley Parker
That's great. _____?
10:48

Ben Hogan
I'll write an evaluation form and HR will assess it and make a decision.
10:49

① What's the process of employee termination
② How can I streamline the hiring process
③ Who was in charge of the hiring process
④ What's gonna happen at the next stage

110 밑줄 친 부분에 들어갈 말로 가장 적절한 것은?

On putting my pricey camera on a seemingly _____ tripod, which looked solid and well-built, three legs of it broke all at once.

① sturdy ② fragile
③ flexible ④ various

109 밑줄 친 부분에 들어갈 말로 가장 적절한 것은?

① 직원 해고 절차가 어떤 거야
② 내가 채용 절차를 어떻게 간소화할 수 있지
③ 누가 채용 절차를 담당하고 있지

어휘 organized 체계적인 good fit 적임자 genuinely 진심으로
evaluation 평가 HR (human resources) 인사팀
assess 평가하다 termination 해고 streamline 간소화하다
in charge of ~을 담당하는

정답 ④

110

해석 내 값비싼 카메라를 언뜻 튼튼해 보이는 삼각대에 놓자마자, 그것은 단단하고 튼튼해 보였는데, 그것(삼각대)의 다리 세 개가 한꺼번에 부서졌다.

어휘 on -ing ~하자마자 pricey 값비싼
seemingly 언뜻 보기에, 겉보기에 tripod 삼각대 solid 단단한
well-built 튼튼한 all at once 한꺼번에, 동시에 sturdy 튼튼한
fragile 약한 flexible 유연한 various 다양한

근거

> On putting my pricey camera on a seemingly sturdy tripod, which looked solid and well-built, three legs of it broke all at once.

정답 ①

주요 어휘 정리

sturdy 튼튼한
= robust
  powerful
  strong

fragile 약한, 깨지기 쉬운
= breakable
  weak
  brittle
  feeble
  frail

flexible 유연한 / 융통성 있는
= elastic   pliable
  resilient   plastic
  supple / adaptable

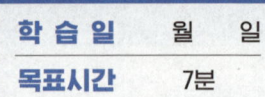

111 밑줄 친 부분에 들어갈 말로 가장 적절한 것은?

> His extravagant and boasting personality has led him to buy the _____ house which is the most expensive and largest in the area.

① frugal ② sparse
③ meager ④ lavish

112 밑줄 친 부분에 들어갈 말로 가장 적절한 것은?

> She was chosen to _____ her country in the upcoming international conference, where she showcased her expertise in diplomacy and economics.

① mislead ② exploit
③ represent ④ encompass

113 밑줄 친 부분에 들어갈 말로 가장 적절한 것은?

> A: Hey! That truck just ran a red light and hit that taxi!
>
> B: Oh no! Is anyone hurt?
>
> A: I was so freaked out that I couldn't check on the drivers.
>
> B: _____
>
> A: Yeah! They assured me that an ambulance would come here very soon.
>
> B: I hope the taxi driver is OK.
>
> A: Hope everyone is fine. I have to hang up now.
>
> B: All right, bye.

① At least, you called 911 and had them get help, right?
② Oh my god, did you try to chase down the truck?
③ You should write down all the details of the accident.
④ As far as I know you used to drive an ambulance.

문장 분석 및 해설

111

해석 그의 사치스럽고 자랑하는 성격은 그가 그 지역에서 가장 비싸고 큰 호화로운 집을 사도록 했다.

어휘 extravagant 사치스러운　boasting 자랑하는　personality 성격
frugal 절약하는　sparse 희박한　meager 메마른
lavish 호화로운

근거

> His extravagant and boasting personality has led him to buy the lavish house which is the most expensive and largest in the area.

정답 ④

주요 어휘 정리

lavish 호화로운
= wasteful
　prodigal
　extravagant
　luxurious

frugal 검소한
= thrifty
　economical

112

해석 그녀는 다가오는 국제회의에서 그녀의 나라를 대표하도록 선택되었고 거기서 그녀는 외교와 경제 분야에서 그녀의 전문성을 보여주었다.

어휘 upcoming 다가오는　international 국제의　conference 회의
showcase 보여주다　expertise 전문성　diplomacy 외교
mislead 호도하다, 잘못 인도하다　exploit 이용하다
represent 대표하다　encompass 포함하다

근거

> She was chosen to represent her country in the upcoming international conference, where she showcased her expertise in diplomacy and economics.

정답 ③

주요 어휘 정리

encompass 포함하다
= include
　involve
　contain
　comprise

exploit 이용하다
= take advantage of

113 밑줄 친 부분에 들어갈 말로 가장 적절한 것은?

> A: 저기! 저 트럭이 방금 빨간불인데 달리다가 저 택시를 들이받았어!
> B: 아 안 돼! 다친 사람은 없니?
> A: 내가 너무 놀라서 운전자들이 괜찮은지 살펴보지 못했어.
> B: 적어도, 911에 전화해서 그들이 도움을 받게 한 거지, 그렇지?
> A: 응! 그들은 구급차가 이리로 곧 올 거라고 장담했어.
> B: 택시 기사님이 괜찮으시길 바라.
> A: 모두들 괜찮으시길. 이제 전화 끊어야 해.
> B: 알았어, 안녕.

② 세상에, 그 트럭을 추적하려고 해봤니?
③ 너는 그 사고의 모든 세부 사항을 적어야만 해.
④ 내가 알기로 너는 한때 구급차를 운전했었어.

어휘 freak out ~을 놀라게 하다　check on (이상이 없는지) 살펴보다
assure 장담하다　hang up 전화를 끊다
chase down ~을 추적하다

정답 ①

DAY 12

114 밑줄 친 부분에 들어갈 말로 가장 적절한 것은?

> A: I've been feeling frustrated lately because of the lack of communication in our team.
> B: I get that. Communication is crucial for our success.
> A: Exactly. We really need clearer guidelines on project updates.
> B: What do you have in mind?
> A: We could have a weekly status meeting.
> B: _____
> A: I think team members take turns giving a presentation to inform others of the status of the project.
> B: Aha, it also helps the team stay on track for a project timeline, then.

① Our team also had a Monday meeting.
② I found myself in a complicated status.
③ How do you expect the meeting to go?
④ Who came up with the new guidelines?

115 밑줄 친 부분에 들어갈 말로 가장 적절한 것은?

> Because working-class people tend to have lower incomes and thus they don't see any particular way to soften the impact of rising prices, they just _____ when inflation remains high.

① revoke ② endure
③ change ④ perish

116 밑줄 친 부분에 들어갈 말로 가장 적절한 것은?

> During their work, they neither talk nor sing, but seem to be determined to _____ their task, for which they are generally paid by the job. They usually make decent money after the work is done.

① resent ② prioritize
③ finish ④ initiate

114 밑줄 친 부분에 들어갈 말로 가장 적절한 것은?

> A: 요즘 우리 팀에서 소통이 잘 안돼서 답답해요.
> B: 이해해요. 우리의 성공을 위해서는 의사소통이 중요해요.
> A: 맞아요. 프로젝트 업데이트에 대한 더 명확한 지침이 필요해요.
> B: 어떤 점을 염두에 두고 계신가요?
> A: 주간 상황 회의를 할 수 있을 것 같아요.
> B: 회의가 어떻게 진행될 거로 예상하세요?
> A: 팀원들이 교대로 프레젠테이션을 해서 프로젝트의 상황을 다른 사람들에게 알리면 될 것 같아요.
> B: 아하, 그러면, 팀이 프로젝트 일정을 계획대로 해나가는 데에도 도움이 되겠네요.

① 우리 팀도 월요일 회의를 했어요.
② 저는 복잡한 상황에 빠졌어요.
④ 누가 새로운 지침을 생각해 냈어요?

어휘 frustrated 답답한 lack 부족 status 상황
take turns 교대로 하다 stay on track 계획대로 하다
complicated 복잡한 come up with ~을 생각해 내다

정답 ③

115

해석 노동자 계층의 사람들은 소득이 더 낮고 따라서 물가 상승의 영향을 완화할 어떤 뾰족한 방법도 보이지 않기 때문에, 인플레이션이 높은 상태일 때 그들은 그냥 <u>견딘다</u>.

어휘 soften 완화시키다 impact 영향 revoke 폐지하다
endure 견디다 change 바꾸다 perish 소멸되다

근거

> Because working-class people tend to have lower incomes and thus they don't see any particular way to soften the impact of rising prices, they just endure when inflation remains high.

정답 ②

주요 어휘 정리
endure 견디다
= withstand
  tolerate
  bear

116

해석 일하는 동안, 그들은 말도 노래도 하지 않고, 그들의 일을 끝내겠다고 단단히 결심한 것으로 보이는데, 그들은 일반적으로 작업 건당으로 보수를 받는다. 그들은 보통 일이 끝난 후에 상당한 돈을 번다.

어휘 determined 단단히 결심한 by the job 작업 건당으로
decent 상당한 resent 분개하다 prioritize 우선순위를 매기다
finish 끝내다 initiate 시작하다

근거

> During their work, they neither talk nor sing, but seem to be determined to finish their task, for which they are generally paid by the job. They usually make decent money after the work is done.

정답 ③

주요 어휘 정리
finish ~을 끝내다
= conclude
  complete
  settle
  go through with

DAY 12

117 밑줄 친 부분에 들어갈 말로 가장 적절한 것은?

A: Hello, I'm calling about the apartment for rent on Oak Street.
B: Would you be interested in seeing the apartment?
A: Yes. I would love to see it.
B: Are you free today at around 5 p.m.?
A: No problem, I will be able to make it then.
B: Well, I'll see you at 5 p.m. Do you know how to get there?
A: _____.
B: You won't need any directions then. The neighborhood hasn't changed much.

① No, I'm not familiar with the area
② Yes, I used to live in that area
③ Oh, I don't have a GPS device on my car
④ Well, I've never been there before

118 밑줄 친 부분에 들어갈 말로 가장 적절한 것은?

A: How's your new job going?
B: It's been challenging but exciting.
A: _____
B: I like the team collaboration and the opportunities to innovate.
A: Sounds like a perfect fit for you. Keep up the good work!
B: Thanks, I really appreciate your support.
A: By the way, if you ever need any advice or support, feel free to reach out.

① How are your coworkers?
② What do you enjoy most about it?
③ Have you considered looking for another job?
④ Do you have any complaints about the company?

문장 분석 및 해설

117 밑줄 친 부분에 들어갈 말로 가장 적절한 것은?

> A: 안녕하세요, 오크 거리에 있는 아파트 임대 때문에 전화드렸습니다.
> B: 아파트를 보시겠어요?
> A: 네. 꼭 보고 싶습니다.
> B: 오늘 오후 5시쯤 시간 괜찮으신가요?
> A: 괜찮아요, 그때 시간 맞춰 갈 수 있을 거예요.
> B: 그럼 오후 5시에 뵙겠습니다. 어떻게 가는지 아시나요?
> A: 네, 제가 그 지역에 살았거든요.
> B: 그러면 길 안내는 필요 없겠네요. 동네가 별로 변한 게 없어요.

① 아뇨, 그 지역은 잘 몰라요
③ 오, 제 차에는 GPS 장비가 없어요
④ 음, 전에 가본 적이 없어요

어휘 rent 임대   make it 시간 맞춰 가다   directions (*pl.*) 길 안내
neighborhood 동네

정답 ②

---

118 밑줄 친 부분에 들어갈 말로 가장 적절한 것은?

> A: 새로운 직장은 어때?
> B: 힘들긴하지만 신나.
> A: 새 직장에서 어떤 것이 가장 좋아?
> B: 팀의 협력 작업과 혁신할 기회가 좋아.
> A: 들어보니 네게 딱 맞는 곳이네. 계속 열심히 해!
> B: 고마워. 네 지원 정말 고마워.
> A: 그런데, 혹시라도 조언이나 지원이 필요하면 부담 갖지 말고 연락해.

① 동료들은 잘 지내?
③ 다른 일 찾아보는 걸 생각해봤니?
④ 회사에 불만 같은 거 있니?

어휘 challenging 힘든   collaboration 협력 작업
innovate 혁신하다   feel free to 부담 없이 ~하다
reach out 연락을 하다   complaint 불만

정답 ②

119 밑줄 친 부분에 들어갈 말로 가장 적절한 것은?

Peter Singer
Mr. Stevens' flight is coming in 30 minutes early this afternoon. I'm heading to pick him up.
10:42

Amy Jones
The team is thrilled he's finally joining us. Is everything set for his welcome meeting?
10:43

Peter Singer
Yes, we've booked the conference room and prepared the agenda.
10:44

Amy Jones
Perfect. I'll ensure the welcome packet and his office are ready. Anything else?
10:45

Peter Singer
_____?
10:46

Amy Jones
Sure, I'll confirm with the IT team right away.
10:47

Peter Singer
Please write down his ID and temporary password.
10:48

① Is his office still undergoing renovations
② Do you have any requests for his office setup
③ Are you aware of his employment conditions
④ Could you check his email has been set up

120 밑줄 친 부분에 들어갈 말로 가장 적절한 것은?

Our team has clearly _____ the disappointment of last week's defeat, saying it was nothing more than a minor hiccup.

① dismissed ② contemplated
③ repaired   ④ retained

119 밑줄 친 부분에 들어갈 말로 가장 적절한 것은?

① 그의 사무실이 아직도 수리 중인가요
② 그의 사무실 설정에 대해 요청할 게 있나요
③ 그의 고용 조건을 알고 계시나요

어휘 head 가다　pick up (자동차로) 마중을 나가다　thrilled 신이 난
conference room 회의실　agenda 안건　ensure 확실하게 하다
packet (선물) 꾸러미　confirm 확인하다　undergo 받다
renovation 수리　be aware of ~을 알다　employment 고용
conditions 조건

정답 ④

120

해석 우리 팀은 지난주의 패배는 사소한 문제에 불과하다고 말하며 그것에 대한 실망감을 확실히 떨쳐 버렸다.

어휘 disappointment 실망, 낙심　defeat 패배
nothing more than ~에 불과한, ~에 지나지 않는
minor 사소한, 작은　hiccup 문제, 딸꾹질
dismiss 떨쳐 버리다　contemplate 곰곰이 생각하다
repair 수리하다　retain 보유하다

근거

> Our team has clearly dismissed the disappointment of last week's defeat, saying it was nothing more than a minor hiccup.

정답 ①

주요 어휘 정리
contemplate ~을 곰곰이 생각하다
= ponder
　ruminate
　muse
　mull over
　meditate
　deliberate

121 밑줄 친 부분에 들어갈 말로 가장 적절한 것은?

> The natives built a(n) _____ castle, so even western invaders with advanced weapons could not conquer them.

① vulnerable ② insecure
③ impregnable ④ standard

122 밑줄 친 부분에 들어갈 말로 가장 적절한 것은?

> One of the hardest conversations you might have at work is one where you have to _____ your word — you can't meet a deadline, you can't help out with a project, you're unable to reach your quarterly goal, and so on.

① keep ② discard
③ continue ④ break

123 밑줄 친 부분에 들어갈 말로 가장 적절한 것은?

> When it comes to moonlighting, it is not always about earning a few more extra bucks. People _____ a second job as a backup when they are insecure about their present job.

① adapt ② extract
③ commence ④ remove

문장 분석 및 해설

121

해석 원주민들은 난공불락의 성을 쌓아서 선진 무기를 가진 서양 침략자들조차 그들을 정복할 수 없었다.

어휘 native 원주민 castle 성 western 서양의 invader 침략자
advanced 선진의 weapon 무기 conquer 정복하다
vulnerable 연약한 insecure 불안정한
impregnable 난공불락의 standard 표준의

근거

> The natives built a(n) impregnable castle, so even western invaders with advanced weapons could not conquer them.

정답 ③

주요 어휘 정리
impregnable 난공불락의, 막강한
= invincible
  unconquerable
  unassailable
  powerful
  tremendous
  formidable

122

해석 직장에서 가장 하기 어려운 대화 중 하나는 약속을 어겨야 하는 대화이다 — 마감일을 맞출 수도 없다거나, 프로젝트에 도움을 줄 수도 없다거나, 분기별 목표를 달성할 수도 없다 등등.

어휘 meet a deadline 마감일을 지키다 help out with ~을 돕다
reach 도달하다, 달성하다 quarterly 분기별의 discard 버리다
break 어기다

근거

> One of the hardest conversations you might have at work is one where you have to break your word — you can't meet a deadline, you can't help out with a project, you're unable to reach your quarterly goal, and so on.

정답 ④

주요 어휘 정리
break one's word 약속을 어기다
keep one's word 약속을 지키다

123

해석 부업에 관한 한, 항상 몇 달러를 더 버는 것과 관련된 것은 아니다. 사람들은 현재 일에 대해 불안할 때 예비용으로서 두 번째 직업을 시작한다.

어휘 moonlighting (야간의) 부업 backup 예비(용) insecure 불안한
adapt 적응하다 extract 추출하다 commence 시작하다
remove 제거하다

근거

> When it comes to moonlighting, it is not always about earning a few more extra bucks. People commence a second job as a backup when they are insecure about their present job.

정답 ③

주요 어휘 정리
commence 시작하다
= begin
  start

124 밑줄 친 부분에 들어갈 말로 가장 적절한 것은?

A: Have you experienced any unusual symptoms lately?
B: Yes, I've been sneezing a lot and my eyes are itching.
A: Have you eaten anything different recently that could trigger allergies?
B: Hmm... I don't think so.
A: It's important to recall any changes in your diet or environment.
B: Actually, now that you mention it, _____ _____.
A: Ah, that could be the trigger. Let's consider allergy testing to confirm.

① I haven't noticed any changes recently
② I did try a new type of nut last week
③ allergies can be triggered by various causes.
④ I haven't eaten anything in a while

125 밑줄 친 부분에 들어갈 말로 가장 적절한 것은?

Both the frogs and toads survived the mass extinction event that _____ the dinosaurs they shared the land with.

① supported   ② contributed
③ exterminated   ④ fortified

126 밑줄 친 부분에 들어갈 말로 가장 적절한 것은?

A: You're soaked in rain. What happened to you?
B: I'm locked out of my apartment.
A: Where did you lose your keys?
B: I think I left them at my job. How could I forget the keys to my own apartment?
A: There is no use in feeling bad about it now. There's nothing you can do about it.
B: You're right. _____
A: Let me go look in my closet. I'll be back in a second.

① Can I stay at your place for a night?
② I should go back at work and find my keys.
③ Do you have some dry clothes I can change into?
④ May I have a glass of hot water?

문장 분석 및 해설

124 밑줄 친 부분에 들어갈 말로 가장 적절한 것은?

> A: 최근에 특별한 증상을 겪지 않았나요?
> B: 네, 재채기를 많이 하고 눈이 가려워요.
> A: 알레르기를 유발할 만한 색다른 것을 최근에 드셨나요?
> B: 음... 그랬던 것 같지 않아요.
> A: 식단이나 환경에 생긴 어떤 변화라도 기억하는 게 중요해요.
> B: 실은, 그 말을 듣고 보니, 지난주에 새로운 종류의 견과류를 먹어 봤어요.
> A: 아, 그게 계기일 수도 있겠네요. 확인해보게 알레르기 검사를 고려해 봅시다.

① 최근에 어떤 변화도 알아차리지 못했어요
③ 알레르기는 다양한 원인으로 유발될 수 있어요
④ 한동안 아무것도 먹지 않았어요

어휘 unusual 특별한 symptom 증상 sneeze 재채기하다
itching 가려운 trigger 유발하다; 계기 recall 기억하다
now that one mention it 그 말을 듣고 보니 mention 말하다
confirm 확인하다 notice 알아차리다

정답 ②

125

해석 개구리와 두꺼비 모두 그들이 땅을 공유했던 공룡들을 없애 버린 대멸종 사건에서 살아남았다.

어휘 toad 두꺼비 survive ~에서 살아남다 extinction 멸종
support 지지하다 contribute 기여하다
exterminate 없애버리다 fortify 강화하다

근거

> Both the frogs and toads survived the mass extinction event that exterminated the dinosaurs they shared the land with.

정답 ③

주요 어휘 정리

exterminate 없애 버리다		fortify 강화하다
= destroy	root out	= strengthen
eradicate	sweep out	reinforce
get rid of	weed out	intensify
wipe out	stamp out	consolidate
		beef up

126 밑줄 친 부분에 들어갈 말로 가장 적절한 것은?

> A: 너 비에 흠뻑 젖었구나. 무슨 일이야?
> B: 내 아파트가 잠겨서 못 들어가.
> A: 열쇠를 어디서 잃어버렸어?
> B: 내 생각에는 회사에 두고 온 것 같아. 어떻게 아파트 열쇠를 잊어버릴 수가 있지?
> A: 그것에 대해 지금 기분 나빠해도 소용없어. 네가 이것에 대해 할 수 있는 일은 없어.
> B: 네 말이 맞아. 내가 갈아입을 수 있는 마른 옷이 있을까?
> A: 옷장을 한 번 볼게. 금방 돌아올게.

① 너의 집에서 하룻밤 신세 질 수 있을까?
② 직장에 돌아가서 열쇠를 찾아야겠어.
④ 따뜻한 물 한 잔 마실 수 있을까?

어휘 soaked 흠뻑 젖은 lock out of 열쇠가 없어서 ~에 못 들어가다
there is no use in ~해도 소용없다
change into ~으로 갈아입다

정답 ③

DAY 13

127 밑줄 친 부분에 들어갈 말로 가장 적절한 것은?

Anna Taylor
Hey, Tim, I just got word that the project deadline has been moved up to Friday.
10:42

Tim Evans
Oh wow, that's sooner than expected.
10:43

Anna Taylor
It is much sooner than expected.
10:44

Tim Evans
Do we need to adjust our schedule?
10:45

Anna Taylor
Yes, let's reschedule the team meeting to tomorrow morning to discuss it.
10:46

Tim Evans
Got it. _____
Anything else?
10:47

Anna Taylor
That should cover it for now. Thanks, Tim!
10:48

① What is the agenda for tomorrow's meeting?
② I'll send out the new meeting invite.
③ Where should we meet?
④ Our schedule has been delayed.

128 밑줄 친 부분에 들어갈 말로 가장 적절한 것은?

A: What's on your mind?
B: Oh. I've been thinking about our upcoming presentation.
A: Is something bothering you about it?
B: Well, I feel like we could add more visuals to make it more engaging.
A: That's a good point. Do you have any ideas?
B: _____
A: That sounds great! By doing so, we can convey complex ideas and make them easier to remember.

① How about using infographics?
② Why don't we discuss it later?
③ We are gathering stacks of ideas.
④ Don't be misled by striking visuals.

127 밑줄 친 부분에 들어갈 말로 가장 적절한 것은?

① 내일 회의 안건은 무엇인가요?
③ 어디서 만날까요?
④ 저희 일정이 지연되었습니다.

어휘 move up (일정을) 앞당기다 adjust 조정하다 agenda 안건
send out 보내다 invite 초대장 delay 연기하다

정답 ②

128 밑줄 친 부분에 들어갈 말로 가장 적절한 것은?

> A: 무슨 걱정 있어요?
> B: 아, 곧 있을 발표에 대해 생각하고 있었어요.
> A: 그것에 대해 무엇이 신경 쓰이세요?
> B: 음, 그걸 더 매력적으로 만들기 위해서 우리가 더 많은 시각 자료를 추가할 수 있을 것 같아서요.
> A: 좋은 지적이네요. 아이디어 있으세요?
> B: 인포그래픽을 사용하는 게 어때요?
> A: 좋은 것 같아요! 그렇게 하면, 복잡한 생각을 전달하고 그것들을 기억하기 쉽게 할 수 있겠네요.

② 나중에 의논하는 게 어때요?
③ 우리는 많은 생각들을 모으고 있어요.
④ 인상적인 시각 자료에 현혹되지 마세요.

어휘 What's on your mind? 무슨 걱정 있어요?
upcoming 곧 있을 presentation 발표 bother 신경 쓰이게 하다
visual 시각 자료 engaging 매력적인 point 지적
convey 전달하다 complex 복잡한 infographic 인포그래픽
gather 모으다 stacks of 많은 mislead 현혹시키다
striking 인상적인

정답 ①

129 밑줄 친 부분에 들어갈 말로 가장 적절한 것은?

Carlos Walker: Lisa, are you ready for the client presentation this afternoon? 10:42

Lisa Lee: Almost. Just finalizing a few slides. What time is the meeting? 10:43

Carlos Walker: It's at 2 PM. 10:44

Lisa Lee: Hmm... are you swamped with work now? 10:45

Carlos Walker: No, I'm pretty open at this point. 10:46

Lisa Lee: I'm wondering _____. 10:47

Carlos Walker: Sure, send them over. I'll check them right away. 10:48

Lisa Lee: Thanks, Carlos. I appreciate it! 10:49

① if you gave the client presentation
② if there's too much to catch up on
③ if you will attend the meeting or not
④ if you can review the big data slides

130 밑줄 친 부분에 들어갈 말로 가장 적절한 것은?

The statement has described the new provisions in the guidelines as vague, _____ and without any due process of law. It seems that the new provisions are far from fair and reasonable.

① incessant
② arbitrary
③ incurable
④ nimble

문장 분석 및 해설

129 밑줄 친 부분에 들어갈 말로 가장 적절한 것은?

① 당신이 고객 프레젠테이션을 했나
② 따라잡아야 할 일이 많은가
③ 당신이 회의에 참석할 건가

어휘 finalize 마무리하다 swamped 무척 바쁜 open 한가한
catch up on ~을 따라잡다

정답 ④

130

해석 그 성명서는 지침의 새로운 조항들이 막연하고, 자의적이고, 정당한 법 절차가 전혀 없다고 설명했다. 새로운 조항은 공정하고 합리적인 것과는 거리가 먼 것 같다.

어휘 statement 성명(서) provision 조항 guideline 지침
vague 모호한 due process of law 정당한 법 절차
incessant 끊임없는 arbitrary 자의적인 incurable 불치의
nimble 기민한

근거

> The statement has described the new provisions in the guidelines as vague, arbitrary and without any due process of law. It seems that the new provisions are far from fair and reasonable.

정답 ②

주요 어휘 정리

incessant 끊임없는	arbitrary 자의적인
= constant	= random
unceasing	
ceaseless	
persistent	

incurable 불치의	nimble 기민한
= untreatable	= shrewd
irremediable	astute
beyond cure	agile
terminal	canny
	speedy
	quick

DAY 13 113

131 밑줄 친 부분에 들어갈 말로 가장 적절한 것은?

> Seeing that he shudders and coughs occasionally, it seems that he is _____.

① ailing ② proficient
③ robust ④ desolate

132 밑줄 친 부분에 들어갈 말로 가장 적절한 것은?

> Many smaller businesses have become _____ because of economic stagnation.

① insolvent ② prosperous
③ lively ④ optimistic

133 밑줄 친 부분에 들어갈 말로 가장 적절한 것은?

> A: The deadline is coming.
> B: I know. We all spare no efforts to get the job done, but running short of time.
> A: We need to think of something to raise efficiency.
> B: Actually, _____
> A: Already? You're really quick at work and on top of things.
> B: You praise me too much. I just tried.
> A: Let's get started now!

① Maybe we should rethink the entire plan.
② I just made out a task delegation table.
③ Have a backup plan if things go wrong?
④ Are you ready for starting from scratch?

문장 분석 및 해설

131

해석 가끔 몸을 떨고 기침하는 걸 보니 그는 병든 것 같다.

어휘 shudder 몸을 떨다　cough 기침하다　occasionally 가끔
ailing 병든　proficient 능숙한　robust 원기 왕성한
desolate 황량한

근거

> Seeing that he shudders and coughs occasionally, it seems that he is ailing.

정답 ①

주요 어휘 정리
ailing 병든
= ill
  unwell
  sick

132

해석 많은 영세사업자들이 경제 침체로 인해 파산했다.

어휘 stagnation 침체　insolvent 파산한　prosperous 번영한, 번창한
lively 생기 넘치는　optimistic 낙관적인

근거

> Many smaller businesses have become insolvent because of economic stagnation.

정답 ①

주요 어휘 정리
insolvent 파산한　　　　prosperous 번영한, 번창한
= bankrupt　　　　　　　= flourishing
  broke　　　　　　　　　　thriving

133 밑줄 친 부분에 들어갈 말로 가장 적절한 것은?

> A: 마감일이 다가와.
> B: 알아. 우리 모두 일을 끝내려고 최선을 다하고 있지만, 시간이 부족해.
> A: 효율을 높이기 위해 뭔가 생각해내야 해.
> B: 실은, 업무 분장표를 그냥 만들어봤어.
> A: 벌써? 너는 정말 일솜씨가 빠르고 뭐든지 잘하는구나.
> B: 과찬이야. 난 그냥 해본 거야.
> A: 이제 시작하자!

① 전체 계획을 다시 생각해 봐야 할 것 같아.
③ 일이 잘못되면 백업 계획이 있니?
④ 처음부터 시작할 각오가 되어 있어?

어휘 deadline 마감일　spare no efforts 최선을 다하다
run short of ~이 부족하다　efficiency 효율
on top of things 뭐든지 잘하는
You praise me too much. 과찬이야.　entire 전체의
go wrong 잘못되다　start from scratch 처음부터 시작하다

정답 ②

DAY 14　115

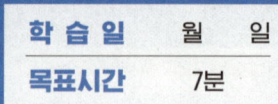

134 밑줄 친 부분에 들어갈 말로 가장 적절한 것은?

> A: We should start preparing dinner soon.
> B: Okay, I'll help chop the vegetables.
> A: Thanks. Could you also set the table?
> B: What's the rush? Dinner isn't for another hour.
> A: _____
> B: You're thoroughly prepared. Okay, I'll do it now.
> A: Perfect. Thanks a lot!

① We will just order takeout instead.
② I just want everything ready before guests arrive.
③ I think we should wait until the guests arrive.
④ Let's do everything last minute to keep it exciting.

135 밑줄 친 부분에 들어갈 말로 가장 적절한 것은?

> Real progress in understanding nature is rarely _____. All important advances are sudden intuitions, new principles, and new ways of seeing.

① incremental   ② abrupt
③ ingenious   ④ turbulent

136 밑줄 친 부분에 들어갈 말로 가장 적절한 것은?

> A: How much did you pay for it?
> B: Almost 600 dollars.
> A: 600 bucks for a piece of junk like that? That's a rip-off!
> B: What do you mean?
> A: _____. You could have found something much better for that price.

① At least it looks nice
② It's not worth it
③ It's a great deal considering the quality
④ It seems like you got a good bargain after all

문장 분석 및 해설

134 밑줄 친 부분에 들어갈 말로 가장 적절한 것은?

> A: 우리 곧 저녁 준비를 시작해야 해.
> B: 알겠어, 내가 채소 써는 것을 도울게.
> A: 고마워. 상도 차려줄 수 있어?
> B: 왜 이렇게 서둘러? 저녁까지 아직 한 시간 정도 남았잖아.
> A: 난 그냥 손님들이 오기 전에 모든 걸 준비해 놓고 싶어.
> B: 넌 준비성이 철저하구나. 좋아, 지금 차릴게.
> A: 완벽해. 정말 고마워!

① 대신 그냥 테이크아웃으로 주문할거야.
③ 손님들이 도착할 때까지 기다려야 할 것 같아.
④ 계속 신나도록 막판에 모든 걸 다 하자.

어휘 prepare 준비하다　chop 썰다　set the table 상을 차리다
What's the rush? 왜 이렇게 서둘러?　last minute 막판에

정답 ②

---

136 밑줄 친 부분에 들어갈 말로 가장 적절한 것은?

> A: 그거 얼마 주고 샀어?
> B: 600달러 가까이 줬어.
> A: 그런 고물을 600달러 주고 샀다고? 바가지 썼군!
> B: 무슨 말이야?
> A: 그 정도 가치는 안 돼. 그 정도 가격이면 훨씬 더 좋은 걸 살 수 있었을 텐데.

① 적어도 좋아 보이긴 해
③ 품질을 고려하면 아주 잘 산 거야
④ 결국 싸게 산 것 같아

어휘 buck 달러, 수사슴　junk 고물, 쓰레기　rip-off 바가지
at least 적어도　worth ~의 가치가 있는　great deal 잘 산 물건
considering ~을 고려하면　bargain 싸게 산 물건　after all 결국

정답 ②

135

해석 자연을 이해하는 것에 있어 진정한 진보는 거의 점진적이지 않다. 모든 중요한 진보는 갑작스러운 직관, 새로운 원리, 그리고 새로운 시각에서 왔다.

어휘 progress 진보　advance 진보　sudden 갑작스러운
incremental 점진적인　abrupt 갑작스러운　ingenious 독창적인
turbulent 사나운

근거
> Real progress in understanding nature is rarely incremental. All important advances are sudden intuitions, new principles, and new ways of seeing.

정답 ①

주요 어휘 정리

incremental 점진적인
= gradual
　progressive

ingenious 독창적인
= original
　innovative
　creative

abrupt 갑작스러운
= sudden

turbulent 사나운
= wild
　violent

DAY 14

137 밑줄 친 부분에 들어갈 말로 가장 적절한 것은?

> His point of view was so well known that he did not have to _____ his opposition to the official position of the city.

① reimburse   ② belittle
③ reiterate   ④ emulate

138 밑줄 친 부분에 들어갈 말로 가장 적절한 것은?

> A: What can I do for you today?
> B: I have a problem with charges on my debit card.
> A: Do you have a statement for your debit card?
> B: Here you are.
> A: What are the charges you're referring to?
> B: The last four charges on the page.
> A: I'm afraid _____.
> B: How long will that take?
> A: I'm not sure, but in the meantime we will freeze these charges.
> B: That's wonderful. Thank you.

① you have to pay a late fee for these charges
② there's nothing we can do for you
③ we're going to have to investigate these charges
④ you cannot evade paying unknown charges

137

해석 그의 관점은 너무 잘 알려져서 그는 시의 공직에 대한 그의 반대 의견을 다시 말할 필요가 없었다.

어휘 opposition 반대, 반목(=disapproval)　reimburse 보상하다
belittle 경시하다　reiterate 다시 말하다　emulate 모방하다

근거

> His point of view was so well known that he did not have to reiterate his opposition to the official position of the city.

정답 ③

주요 어휘 정리

reimburse 보상하다	reiterate 다시 말하다
= compensate	= repeat
remunerate	iterate
reward	restate

138 밑줄 친 부분에 들어갈 말로 가장 적절한 것은?

> A: 오늘 무엇을 도와드릴까요?
> B: 제 직불카드에 청구된 요금에 문제가 있습니다.
> A: 직불카드에 대한 명세서가 있나요?
> B: 여기 있습니다.
> A: 어떤 요금을 말씀하시는 건가요?
> B: 페이지의 마지막 네 가지 요금입니다.
> A: 죄송하지만 이 요금들에 대해 조사를 해야 할 것 같습니다.
> B: 얼마나 걸릴까요?
> A: 확실하지 않습니다, 그러나 그사이에 이 요금을 동결할 것입니다.
> B: 잘됐네요. 감사합니다.

① 이 요금들에 대한 연체료를 지불해야 합니다
② 저희가 할 수 있는 게 없습니다
④ 알 수 없는 요금을 내는 것을 피할 수 없습니다

어휘 charge 요금　debit card 직불카드　statement 명세서
in the meantime 그사이에　freeze 동결하다　a late fee 연체료
investigate 조사하다　evade 피하다

정답 ③

DAY 14

139 밑줄 친 부분에 들어갈 말로 가장 적절한 것은?

Michelle Green: James, have you seen the email about the office party next week? 10:42

James Wood: Yes, I did. Are you planning to attend? 10:43

Michelle Green: Definitely. Are we supposed to bring anything? 10:44

James Wood: It says we can bring snacks or drinks if we want. _____ 10:45

Michelle Green: Sounds good. I'll bring snacks, and you can bring drinks? 10:46

James Wood: Perfect. I'll pick up some drinks on my way in. 10:47

① Let's divide the roles.
② I'll take care of everything.
③ How much did you pay for snacks?
④ What do you prefer to drink?

140 밑줄 친 부분에 들어갈 말로 가장 적절한 것은?

If asked to give any words of advice for young people as a grown-up, I'd like to tell them that they should invest their time and money more into things like knowledge, instead of only into buying _____ things such as fancy-looking bags or shoes.

① incisive
② perennial
③ tangible
④ abstract

문장 분석 및 해설

139 밑줄 친 부분에 들어갈 말로 가장 적절한 것은?

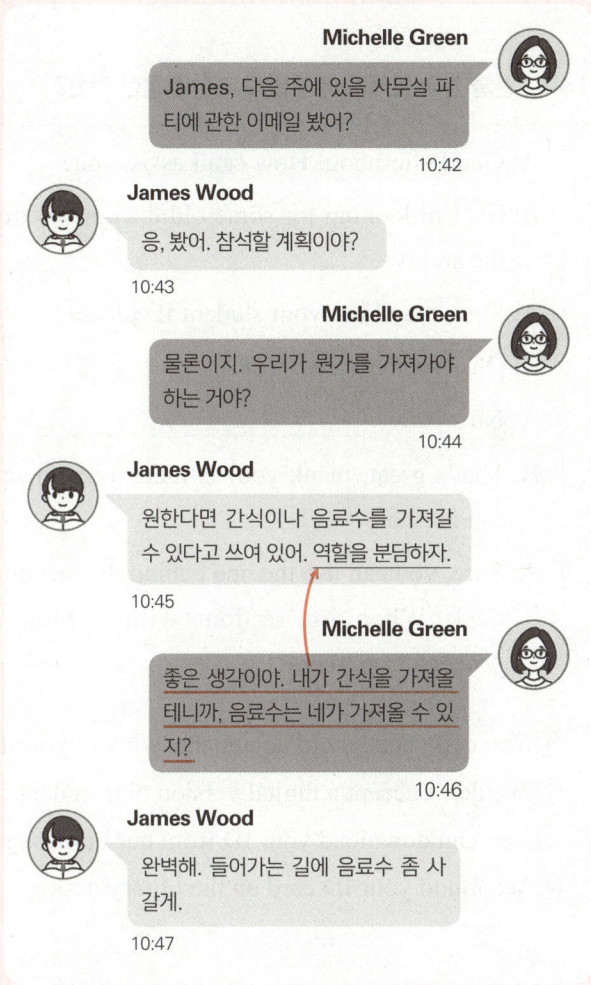

② 내가 다 책임질게.
③ 간식에 얼마를 지불했어?
④ 어떤 음료를 선호해?

어휘 attend 참석하다 pick up 사 가다 take care of ~을 책임지다

정답 ①

140

해석 만일 내가 어른으로서 청년들에게 조언해 줄 것을 요청받으면, 나는 그들에게 멋져 보이는 가방이나 신발과 같은 유형의 것들만 사는 대신 그들의 시간과 돈을 지식과 같은 것에 더 투자하라고 말하고 싶다.

어휘 advice 조언 grown-up 어른 invest 투자하다
knowledge 지식 fancy-looking 멋져 보이는 incisive 예리한
perennial 지속되는 tangible 유형의, 실재하는
abstract 추상적인

근거

> If asked to give any words of advice for young people as a grown-up, I'd like to tell them that they should invest their time and money more into things like knowledge, instead of only into buying tangible things such as fancy-looking bags or shoes.

정답 ③

주요 어휘 정리

incisive 예리한	↔	dull 둔한
= keen		= blunt
sharp		

perennial 지속되는, 영원한	
= lasting	perpetual
everlasting	persistent
continual	incessant
forever	unceasing
permanent	ceaseless

tangible	↔	intangible
유형의, 실재하는		무형의
= real		= abstract
actual		impalpable
concrete		
palpable		

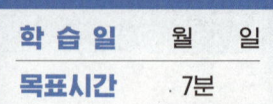

141 밑줄 친 부분에 들어갈 말로 가장 적절한 것은?

> The success of fraudsters often does hinge on their ability to tell a convincing story. They make up pretty _____ stories to get what they want.

① persuasive ② unrealistic
③ frequent   ④ distorted

142 밑줄 친 부분에 들어갈 말로 가장 적절한 것은?

> There are many kinds of businesses. They sell various things. If they suffer a loss in one division, they can _____ for it with a gain in another division.

① search   ② account
③ apply   ④ compensate

143 밑줄 친 부분에 들어갈 말로 가장 적절한 것은?

> A: Good afternoon! How can I assist you?
> B: Hi, I'm looking for some old documents from the archive.
> A: Sure, may I see your student ID please?
> B: Oh, I seem to have lost it.
> A: No worries. _____.
> B: That's great, thank you! Is there a computer I can use here?
> A: Sure, you can use the one behind the reception desk. When you're done with it, you can proceed from there.

① You can't access old documents without your ID
② We don't accept a digital version of a student ID
③ You can download your ID from our homepage
④ We found your ID card on the library desk

141

해석 사기꾼의 성공은 종종 설득력 있는 이야기를 하는 능력에 달려있다. 그들은 자신들이 원하는 것을 얻기 위해 매우 설득력 있는 이야기를 지어낸다.

어휘 fraudster 사기꾼   hinge on ~에 달려 있다
convincing 설득력 있는   make up 지어내다
persuasive 설득력 있는   unrealistic 비현실적인   frequent 잦은
distorted 왜곡된

근거

> The success of fraudsters often does hinge on their ability to tell a convincing story. They make up pretty persuasive stories to get what they want.

정답 ①

주요 어휘 정리
persuasive 설득력 있는
= convincing
  compelling
  influential
  credible

142

해석 다양한 사업체가 있다. 그들은 다양한 것을 판다. 그들은 한 사업부에서 손해를 보면 다른 사업부에서의 이익으로 그것을 만회할 수 있다.

어휘 suffer a loss 손해를 보다   division 부(部)   gain 이익
search for ~을 찾다   account for ~을 설명하다
apply for ~을 신청[지원]하다   compensate for ~을 만회하다

근거

> There are many kinds of businesses. They sell various things. If they suffer a loss in one division, they can compensate for it with a gain in another division.

정답 ④

주요 어휘 정리
compensate for ~을 만회하다
= make up for

143 밑줄 친 부분에 들어갈 말로 가장 적절한 것은?

A: 안녕하세요! 어떻게 도와드릴까요?
B: 안녕하세요, 저는 기록보관소에서 오래된 문서를 구하고 있어요.
A: 그렇군요, 학생증을 보여주시겠어요?
B: 오, 학생증을 잃어버린 것 같아요.
A: 걱정하지 마세요. 우리 홈페이지에서 신분증을 내려받을 수 있어요.
B: 그거 잘됐네요, 고맙습니다! 여기 제가 사용할 수 있는 컴퓨터가 있을까요?
A: 그럼요, 접수대 뒤에 있는 걸 사용하시면 됩니다. 다 되시면, 거기서부터 진행하기로 하죠.

① 신분증이 없으면 오래된 문서를 이용할 수 없어요
② 우리는 디지털 학생증은 받아 주지 않아요
④ 당신 신분증을 도서관 책상에서 발견했어요

어휘 assist 돕다   archive 기록보관소   reception desk 접수대
proceed 진행하다   access 이용하다   accept 받아주다

정답 ③

144 밑줄 친 부분에 들어갈 말로 가장 적절한 것은?

> He always dreams _____ dreams such as becoming a Superman, a Spiderman or other comic heroes.

① reasonable ② objective
③ absurd ④ intelligent

145 밑줄 친 부분에 들어갈 말로 가장 적절한 것은?

> Detectives _____ the suspect's movements using security camera footage.

① discard ② trace
③ nourish ④ miss

146 밑줄 친 부분에 들어갈 말로 가장 적절한 것은?

> A: I'm supposed to meet with you at 1:30.
> B: Yes, I see. What did you need to see me about?
> A: There's a problem with my schedule. _____.
> B: Oh, I see.
> A: Is it at all possible for you to fix that error?
> B: No problem. Let me see if I can find one of these classes on another day.
> A: I would greatly appreciate that.

① Two of my classes occur at the same time
② I signed up too many credits for this semester
③ My math professor is strict in grading
④ I have to take a year off from school

144

해석 그는 항상 슈퍼맨, 스파이더맨, 또는 다른 만화 영웅이 되는 것과 같은 터무니없는 꿈을 꾼다.

어휘 comic 만화 reasonable 타당한 objective 객관적인
absurd 터무니없는 intelligent 똑똑한

근거

> He always dreams absurd dreams such as becoming a Superman, a Spiderman or other comic heroes.

정답 ③

주요 어휘 정리
absurd 터무니없는
= ridiculous
  ludicrous
  nonsensical
  preposterous

145

해석 형사는 보안 카메라 화면을 이용해 용의자의 움직임을 추적한다.

어휘 detective 형사 suspect 용의자 movement 움직임
security 보안 footage (특정한 사건을 담은) 화면 discard 버리다
trace 추적하다 nourish 영양을 주다 miss 놓치다

근거

> Detectives trace the suspect's movements using security camera footage.

정답 ②

주요 어휘 정리
trace 추적하다
= track
  monitor
  follow
  investigate

146 밑줄 친 부분에 들어갈 말로 가장 적절한 것은?

> A: 1시 반에 당신과 면담하기로 되어 있는데요.
> B: 네, 그렇군요. 무슨 일 때문에 저를 보자 하셨죠?
> A: 제 시간표에 문제가 있어서요. 제 수업 중에 두 수업이 같은 시간에 있습니다.
> B: 아, 그렇군요.
> A: 이 오류를 해결하실 수 있을까요?
> B: 문제없어요. 이 수업 중 하나가 다른 날에도 있는지 볼게요.
> A: 그래 주시면 대단히 감사하겠습니다.

② 이번 학기에 너무 많은 학점을 신청했어요
③ 제 수학 교수님이 평가에 엄격해요
④ 1년 휴학을 해야 해요

어휘 schedule 시간표 sign up 신청하다 credit 학점 strict 엄격한 grading 평가

정답 ①

147 밑줄 친 부분에 들어갈 말로 가장 적절한 것은?

Sarah Johnson: Hi, I'd like to place an order for groceries. 10:42

Green Valley Grocers: Sure, please choose the items you'd like from the list I sent you. 10:43

Sarah Johnson: I've just made my selections. 10:44

Green Valley Grocers: Okay. _____. 10:45

Sarah Johnson: Why not deliver it now? 10:46

Green Valley Grocers: I apologize, but our instant delivery service is only available until 7 pm, and it's currently 7:20 pm. 10:47

Sarah Johnson: I understand. Thank you for arranging the delivery. 10:48

① We will deliver the items you have ordered promptly
② Your order will be delivered as soon as they are restocked
③ Please specify the delivery date that works best for you
④ Your order will be delivered tomorrow morning by 10 am

148 밑줄 친 부분에 들어갈 말로 가장 적절한 것은?

A: Can you believe we're about to graduate?
B: I know, it's unbelievable! Congratulations!
A: Thank you. Same to you.
B: By the way, I wonder _____.
A: According to the schedule, about four hours.
B: I'm going to cherish every minute of this event.
A: That's the spirit.

① when we can receive our diplomas
② how long the commencement is going to be
③ what your plans are after this
④ how long it took you to graduate

147 밑줄 친 부분에 들어갈 말로 가장 적절한 것은?

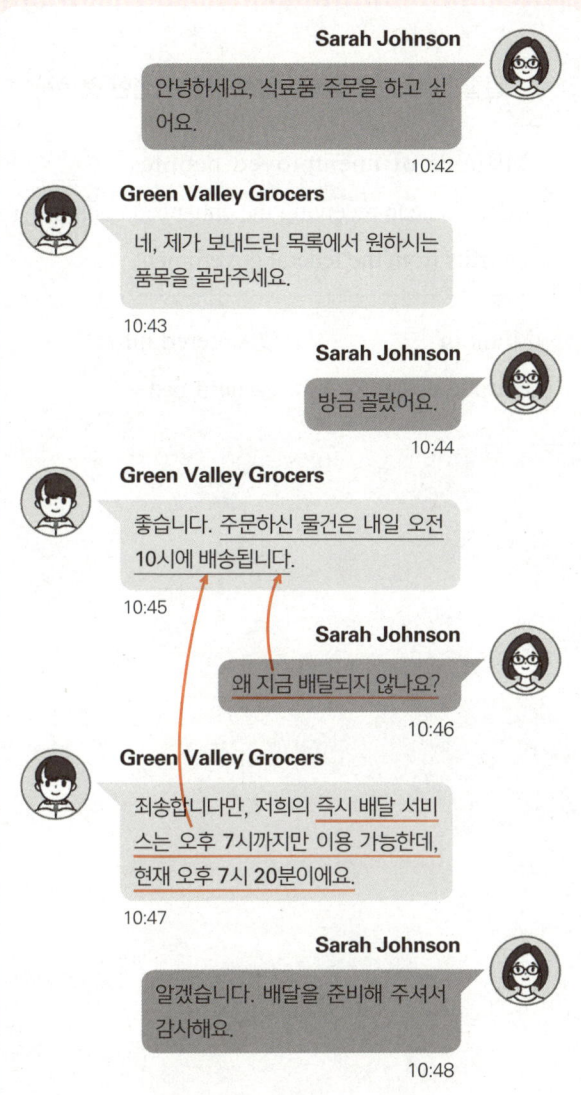

① 주문하신 품목을 즉시 배달하겠습니다
② 주문은 물품이 다시 채워지는 즉시 배달해드릴게요
③ 당신에게 가장 잘 맞는 배달 날짜를 구체적으로 말해주세요

어휘 grocery 식료품   item 품목   apologize 사과하다   instant 즉시의
available 이용 가능한   currently 현재   arrange 준비하다
promptly 즉시   restock 다시 채우다   specify 구체적으로 말하다

정답 ④

148 밑줄 친 부분에 들어갈 말로 가장 적절한 것은?

A: 우리가 곧 졸업한다는 게 믿어지니?
B: 맞아, 믿을 수 없어! 축하해!
A: 고마워. 너도.
B: 그나저나, 학위 수여식이 얼마나 걸릴지 궁금해.
A: 일정에 따르면, 약 4시간 정도야.
B: 나는 이 행사의 매 순간을 소중히 여길 거야.
A: 바로 그거야.

① 언제 우리가 졸업장을 받을지
③ 이 이후에 너의 계획이 무엇인지
④ 네가 졸업하는 데 얼마나 걸렸는지

어휘 by the way 그나저나   cherish 소중히 여기다
that's the spirit 바로 그거다(잘했다고 칭찬하는 말)
diploma 졸업장   commencement 학위 수여식

정답 ②

149 밑줄 친 부분에 들어갈 말로 가장 적절한 것은?

Emma Davies
Hey, Luke, did you know it's Karen's birthday tomorrow?
10:42

Luke Hall
Really? I didn't realize. Are we doing something for her?
10:43

Emma Davies
Yes, I was thinking of getting a cake and some decorations. Want to help?
10:44

Luke Hall
Absolutely. _____ _____.
10:45

Emma Davies
I'll get the cake, then. Let's meet early tomorrow to set everything up.
10:46

Luke Hall
Sounds like a plan. See you then!
10:47

① I'll buy a cake on my way there
② I haven't decided what to get for her
③ I'll take care of the decorations
④ I'm the last person to tell anybody

150 밑줄 친 부분에 들어갈 말로 가장 적절한 것은?

Millions of unemployed people _____ job offers to keep receiving the enhanced unemployment benefits from the federal government.

① took in
② entered into
③ turned down
④ held fast to

149 밑줄 친 부분에 들어갈 말로 가장 적절한 것은?

① 거기로 가는 길에 케이크를 살게
② 그녀를 위해 무엇을 사야 할지 결정하지 못했어
④ 난 절대 아무에게도 말할 사람 아냐

어휘 decoration 장식(품) Sounds like a plan. 좋은 생각이야.
take care of ~을 책임지다 set up 준비하다
the last person to (tell) 절대 (말)하지 않을 사람

정답 ③

150

해석 수백만의 실업자들은 연방정부로부터 강화된 실업 수당을 계속해서 받기 위해 일자리 제의를 거절했다.

어휘 unemployed 실직한 enhance 강화하다
unemployment benefit 실업 수당
take in 받아들이다, 속이다, 구독하다 enter into 시작하다
turn down 거절하다 hold fast to 고수하다

근거

> Millions of unemployed people turned down job offers to keep receiving the enhanced unemployment benefits from the federal government.

정답 ③

주요 어휘 정리

take in
= accept 받아들이다
  deceive 속이다
  subscribe 구독하다
  comprehend, understand 이해하다
  intake, ingest 섭취하다

enter into 시작하다
= go into

turn down 거절하다
= veto
  refuse

hold fast to 고수하다
= hang on to
  adhere to
  stick to
  cling to

151 밑줄 친 부분에 들어갈 말로 가장 적절한 것은?

> We need to learn how to repair and _____ the Earth's ozone layer, which is destroyed by human.

① exhaust ② replenish
③ empty   ④ harness

152 밑줄 친 부분에 들어갈 말로 가장 적절한 것은?

> The botanical garden can _____ colorful life of its own. The cooler weather allows heat-dormant plants to come alive again and spread their fresh color over the garden.

① delay   ② assume
③ deliver ④ crave

153 밑줄 친 부분에 들어갈 말로 가장 적절한 것은?

> A: Would you like to order anything else?
> B: No, I'm stuffed. All we need now is our check.
> A: Let me take care of this bill. You treated me last time.
> B: _____
> A: All right, let me buy you coffee, instead.

① How about paying for what each of us ate?
② I think it's too expensive to pay on my own.
③ Why don't you treat me to dinner today?
④ Please, take care of yourself when you feel low.

문장 분석 및 해설

151

해석 우리는 인간에 의해 파괴되는 지구의 오존층을 복구하고 보충하는 방법을 배울 필요가 있다.

어휘 repair 복구하다   ozone layer 오존층   destroy 파괴하다
exhaust 기진맥진하게 만들다   replenish 보충하다   empty 비우다
harness 이용하다

근거

> We need to learn how to repair and replenish the Earth's ozone layer, which is destroyed by human.

정답 ②

주요 어휘 정리
replenish 보충하다
= refill
  supplement
  make up for

152

해석 식물원은 자체의 다채로운 활기를 띨 수 있다. 더 서늘해진 날씨는 여름 휴면 중인 식물이 다시 활기를 띠고 정원에 그들의 밝은 색을 퍼트릴 수 있게 해준다.

어휘 botanical garden 식물원   life 활기
heat-dormant 여름 휴면 중인   come alive 활기를 띠다
fresh (색이) 밝은   delay 지연시키다   assume 띠다
deliver 배달하다   crave 열망하다

근거

> The botanical garden can assume colorful life of its own. The cooler weather allows heat-dormant plants to come alive again and spread their fresh color over the garden.

정답 ②

주요 어휘 정리
assume 띠다   crave 열망하다
= take on   = long for
                         yearn for
                         aspire
                         desire

153 밑줄 친 부분에 들어갈 말로 가장 적절한 것은?

> A: 다른 거 더 주문할래?
> B: 아니, 나 배불러. 지금 우리가 필요한 건 계산서야.
> A: 이 계산서는 내가 낼게. 지난번에 네가 대접했잖아.
> B: 각자 먹은 걸 계산하는 게 어때?
> A: 좋아, 대신, 커피는 내가 사게 해줘.

② 내가 혼자 내기에는 너무 비싼 것 같아.
③ 오늘 저녁을 나한테 대접하는 게 어때?
④ 기운이 없을 때는 몸을 잘 돌보세요.

어휘 stuffed 배가 부른   treat 대접하다   expensive 비싼
on one's own 혼자서   feel low 기운이 없다

정답 ①

DAY 16   131

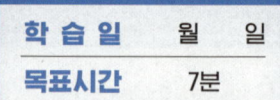

154 밑줄 친 부분에 들어갈 말로 가장 적절한 것은?

> A: Hey, did you hear about what happened to Bob?
> B: No, what happened to him?
> A: I heard he got fired last week. That's why no one has seen him around the office anymore.
> B: Are you sure about that? You shouldn't always believe what you hear.
> A: _____.
> B: Maybe he's on vacation.
> A: I hope you're right. Bob is a nice guy.

① He's been absent since last Wednesday
② He has many explanations for it
③ He has been in Hawaii on vacation
④ I just happened to see him

155 밑줄 친 부분에 들어갈 말로 가장 적절한 것은?

> There is a(n) _____ between these two data. So we need to find out what's difference and correct it right now.

① discrepancy   ② antipathy
③ supremacy   ④ virtue

156 밑줄 친 부분에 들어갈 말로 가장 적절한 것은?

> Please keep this roller coaster safety tip in mind. If your wallet or cell phone falls off from your pocket, don't try to _____ it. An impulsive reaction to get hold of the wallet or phone can result in accidents. Let it go, literally.

① retrieve   ② extract
③ irrigate   ④ discharge

154 밑줄 친 부분에 들어갈 말로 가장 적절한 것은?

> A: 이봐, Bob에게 무슨 일이 있는지 들었어?
> B: 아니, 그가 어떻게 됐는데?
> A: 그가 지난주에 해고되었다고 들었어. 그래서 사무실에서 아무도 그를 더 이상 보지 못한 거야.
> B: 그거 확실해? 들었다고 항상 믿으면 안 돼.
> A: <u>그는 지난 수요일부터 결근했어.</u>
> B: 휴가 중일 수 있지.
> A: 네 말이 맞길 바라. Bob은 좋은 사람이야.

② 그는 여러 이유를 댈 수 있어
③ 그는 휴가차 하와이에 다녀왔어
④ 방금 그를 우연히 봤어

어휘 fire 해고하다 absent 결근한 happen to 우연히 ~하다

정답 ①

155

해석 이 두 데이터에는 차이가 있다. 그래서 우리는 즉시 차이가 무엇인지를 알아내고 수정할 필요가 있다.

어휘 trust 신뢰하다 discrepancy 차이 antipathy 반감
supremacy 우위 virtue 미덕

근거

> There is a(n) <u>discrepancy</u> between these two data. So we need to find out what's difference and correct it right now.

정답 ①

주요 어휘 정리

discrepancy 차이
= difference
  disparity
  disagreement

antipathy 반감
= aversion
  dislike
  animosity
  loathing
  hostility

156

해석 이 롤러코스터 안전 팁을 명심해 주세요. 주머니에서 지갑이나 휴대폰이 떨어져 나간다면 되찾으려고 하지 말아 주세요. 지갑이나 휴대폰을 잡기 위한 충동적인 반응은 사고로 이어질 수 있습니다. 말 그대로 그냥 보내주시기 바랍니다.

어휘 wallet 지갑 impulsive 충동적인 get hold of ~을 잡다
result in ~로 이어지다 accident 사고 literally 말 그대로
retrieve 되찾다 extract 발췌하다 irrigate (땅에) 물을 대다
discharge 방출하다

근거

> Please keep this roller coaster safety tip in mind. If your wallet or cell phone falls off from your pocket, don't try to <u>retrieve</u> it. An impulsive reaction to get hold of the wallet or phone can result in accidents. Let it go, literally.

정답 ①

주요 어휘 정리
retrieve 되찾다
= recover
  restore
  revitalize
  get back

157 밑줄 친 부분에 들어갈 말로 가장 적절한 것은?

> A: Hey Jack. You look tired. What's going on?
> B: It's finals week and I have been up all night studying.
> A: How many exams do you have left?
> B: Three more to go.
> A: Haven't you been keeping up your studies?
> B: _____
> A: Looks like you'll be in for a tough week.

① You are the last person to study hard.
② If you were me, would you keep up?
③ Staying up late is bad for your health.
④ If I have, wouldn't I need to stay up?

158 밑줄 친 부분에 들어갈 말로 가장 적절한 것은?

> Among his numberless works, not a single one was appreciated as a masterpiece though he had been consistently _____ in writing novels and poems.

① fruitless
② vague
③ prolific
④ obvious

157 밑줄 친 부분에 들어갈 말로 가장 적절한 것은?

> A: 이 봐 Jack. 피곤해 보이네. 무슨 일이야?
> B: 이번 주가 기말고사 주간이라 공부하느라 밤을 새우고 있어.
> A: 시험이 몇 개나 남았는데?
> B: 앞으로 세 개 더.
> A: 공부를 꾸준히 해오지 않았어?
> B: 내가 그랬으면, 밤을 새울 필요가 없지 않겠어?
> A: 힘든 한 주를 보내겠구나.

① 넌 공부를 절대 안 할 사람이야.
② 네가 나라면, 꾸준히 하겠어?
③ 늦게까지 깨어있는 건 건강에 좋지 않아.

어휘 keep up ~을 꾸준히 하다   tough 힘든
the last person to ~을 절대 안 할 사람

정답 ④

158

해석 비록 그는 소설과 시 창작에서 꾸준히 다작해왔지만 그의 무수히 많은 작품 중에서, 단 하나도 걸작으로 인정받지 못했다.

어휘 numberless 무수히 많은   appreciate 인정하다
masterpiece 걸작   consistently 꾸준히   novel 소설   poem 시
fruitless 성과 없는   vague 모호한   prolific 다작의
obvious 확실한

근거
> Among his numberless works, not a single one was appreciated as a masterpiece though he had been consistently prolific in writing novels and poems.

정답 ③

주요 어휘 정리

vague 모호한	↔	obvious 분명한
= ambiguous		= apparent
indistinct		distinct
uncertain		certain
obscure		

fruitless 성과 없는, 불모의	↔	prolific 다작의, 다산의, 비옥한
= unproductive		= productive
infertile		fertile
unfruitful		fruitful

159 밑줄 친 부분에 들어갈 말로 가장 적절한 것은?

> A: We're running late for the movie.
> B: I know, traffic's terrible.
> A: Step on it. We're going to miss the beginning.
> B: I'm trying, but these cars aren't moving.
> A: Do you have any good idea?
> B: _____.
> A: I heard its construction has been completed. That'll get us there faster.

① The side streets should have been mended quickly
② I think we should give up going to the theater
③ I would rather be late than not get there at all
④ Let's take a detour and pass the newly-built tunnel

160 밑줄 친 부분에 들어갈 말로 가장 적절한 것은?

Mia Barns
Where are you planning to hold your party this time?
10:42

Bill Brison
I don't know. I used to hold the Christmas party at a fancy restaurant.
10:43

Mia Barns
Yeah, that was fantastic.
10:44

Bill Brison
But it always cost an arm and a leg.
10:45

Mia Barns
You're absolutely right. _____
10:46

Bill Brison
Great idea! That way, we can save money and everybody will admire my plants.
10:47

① Why don't you stick to a fancy restaurant?
② I can't go to the party because I hurt my leg.
③ How about holding a simple garden party?
④ It will be very hard to satisfy everyone.

159 밑줄 친 부분에 들어갈 말로 가장 적절한 것은?

> A: 영화에 늦겠어.
> B: 맞아, 교통체증이 심해.
> A: 속도를 내봐, 시작 부분을 놓치겠어.
> B: 노력하고 있는데, 이 차들이 움직이질 않아.
> A: 좋은 생각 있어?
> B: 우회해서 새로 세운 터널을 통과하자.
> A: 그것의 건설이 완성되었다는 건 들었어. 그러면 더 빨리 도착하겠다.

① 옆길은 빠르게 수리되었어야 해.
② 극장 가는 건 포기하는 게 좋을 것 같아
③ 거기 아예 못 가느냐 늦게 가는 게 낫지

어휘 run late 늦다 traffic 교통 Step on it. 속도를 내봐.
construction 건설 complete 완성하다 mend 수리하다
take a detour 우회하다

정답 ④

160 밑줄 친 부분에 들어갈 말로 가장 적절한 것은?

① 고급 식당을 고수하는 게 어때?
② 나는 다리를 다쳐서 파티에 갈 수 없어.
④ 모두를 만족시키는 건 아주 어려울 거야.

어휘 fancy 고급의 cost an arm and a leg 엄청난 돈이 들다
absolutely 전적으로 throw a party 파티를 열다
stick to ~을 고수하다 satisfy 만족시키다

정답 ③

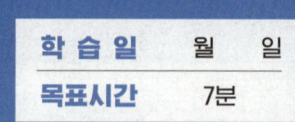

161. 밑줄 친 부분에 들어갈 말로 가장 적절한 것은?

> Social media is being used to _____ public opinion around the world, a study from the University of Oxford has revealed. The study finds widespread use of social media for promoting lies, misinformation and propaganda by governments and individuals.

① supplant
② elucidate
③ condense
④ manipulate

162. 밑줄 친 부분에 들어갈 말로 가장 적절한 것은?

> While using the tool may be _____ at first, persistent practice will help you use it to your advantage.

① convenient
② awkward
③ comfortable
④ beneficial

163. 밑줄 친 부분에 들어갈 말로 가장 적절한 것은?

> A: I had a wonderful time at dinner tonight.
> B: Me too! The food was excellent.
> A: So, shall we ask for the bill?
> B: Sure. Let's split it.
> A: I will treat you tonight.
> B: Are you sure? That's very kind of you.
> A: And _____
> B: Right. We should take turns.

① you can get the tab the next.
② you should make a right turn.
③ I will go to the restaurant with you.
④ I will buy you some food next week.

161

해석 소셜 미디어가 전 세계적으로 여론을 조작하기 위해 사용되고 있다고 옥스퍼드 대학의 한 연구는 밝혔다. 이 연구는 정부와 개인에 의한 거짓말, 잘못된 정보 및 선전을 홍보하기 위해 소셜 미디어가 널리 사용되고 있음을 밝힌다.

어휘 public opinion 여론   reveal 밝히다
misinformation 잘못된 정보
propaganda (허위·과장된 정치) 선전   supplant 대신하다
elucidate 설명하다   condense 압축하다   manipulate 조작하다

근거

> Social media is being used to manipulate public opinion around the world, a study from the University of Oxford has revealed. The study finds widespread use of social media for promoting lies, misinformation and propaganda by governments and individuals.

정답 ④

주요 어휘 정리

supplant 대신[대체]하다
= replace
  supersede
  substitute
  take the place of

condense (글·정보를) 압축하다
= abridge
  shorten

manipulate 조작하다
= control
  exploit

162

해석 처음에는 그 도구를 사용하는 것이 서투를 수 있지만, 지속적인 연습은 그것을 당신에게 유리하게 사용할 수 있도록 도와줄 것이다.

어휘 tool 도구   persistent 지속적인   practice 연습
to one's advantage (~에게) 유리하게   convenient 편리한
awkward 서투른   comfortable 편안한   beneficial 유익한

근거

> While using the tool may be awkward at first, persistent practice will help you use it to your advantage.

정답 ②

주요 어휘 정리

awkward 서투른
= unskilled
  clumsy
  inept

163 밑줄 친 부분에 들어갈 말로 가장 적절한 것은?

> A: 오늘 저녁 식사는 정말 즐거웠어요.
> B: 저도요! 음식이 훌륭했어요.
> A: 그럼 계산서를 달라고 할까요?
> B: 그러죠. 나눠서 냅시다.
> A: 오늘 밤은 제가 한턱낼게요.
> B: 정말요? 정말 고마워요.
> A: 그리고 다음번에는 당신이 계산하면 되잖아요.
> B: 그래요. 우리 번갈아 가면서 계산해요.

② 너는 우회전을 해야 해.
③ 당신하고 그 식당에 갈게요.
④ 다음 주에 음식을 살게요.

어휘 excellent 훌륭한   bill 계산서   split (몫을) 나누다   treat 한턱내다
absolutely 그럼(강한 동의를 나타냄)   pick up the tab 계산하다
take turns 번갈아가면서 하다

정답 ①

164 밑줄 친 부분에 들어갈 말로 가장 적절한 것은?

> Experts say, to be truly _____, you need to be actively prepared for change and be consistently developing more skills in order to meet emerging needs.

① adaptable ② lucrative
③ arrogant ④ mandatory

165 밑줄 친 부분에 들어갈 말로 가장 적절한 것은?

> As unskilled labor positions become more and more _____, workers will be forced to acquire new skills to compete.

① selfish ② astute
③ obsolete ④ bitter

166 밑줄 친 부분에 들어갈 말로 가장 적절한 것은?

> A: Could I buy a bus pass today?
> B: Which bus pass would you like to purchase?
> A: Can you tell me my options?
> B: There are passes for a day, month, and week, and there are student passes.
> A: _____?
> B: It's free for the pass, but the monthly sticker is $12.
> A: I'll take it then.
> B: Sure, can I see your student ID?
> A: Sure, here you are.

① What's the penalty for a free ride
② Which one is the most reasonable
③ How much does the student pass cost
④ Are there any restrictions on an extension

문장 분석 및 해설

164

해석 전문가들은 진정으로 (새로운 환경에) 적응할 수 있으려면, 적극적으로 변화에 준비되어 있어야 하고 새로운 요구를 충족시킬 수 있도록 더 많은 기술을 지속적으로 개발해야 한다고 말한다.

어휘
consistently 지속적으로 emerging 새로운
adaptable 적응할 수 있는 lucrative 수익성이 좋은
arrogant 거만한 mandatory 의무적인

근거

> Experts say, to be truly adaptable, you need to be actively prepared for change and be consistently developing more skills in order to meet emerging needs.

정답 ①

주요 어휘 정리

adaptable 적응할 수 있는
= flexible
  resilient
  adjustable

lucrative 수익성이 좋은
= profitable
  money-making
  gainful

arrogant 거만한
= haughty
  supercilious
  stuck-up
  pompous
  condescending

mandatory 의무적인
= compulsory
  obligatory
  requisite
  forced
  required

165

해석 기술이 필요하지 않은 노동직이 점점 더 구식이 됨에 따라, 노동자들은 경쟁하기 위해 새로운 기술을 습득해야 할 것이다.

어휘
unskilled 기술이 필요하지 않은 acquire 습득하다
compete 경쟁하다 selfish 이기적인 astute 기민한
obsolete 구식의 bitter 격렬한

근거

> As unskilled labor positions become more and more obsolete, workers will be forced to acquire new skills to compete.

정답 ③

주요 어휘 정리

obsolete 구식의 ↔ up-to-date 최신의
= outdated   = updated
  old-fashioned
  out of date

astute 기민한
= agile   shrewd
  canny   speedy
  nimble   rapid

166 밑줄 친 부분에 들어갈 말로 가장 적절한 것은?

> A: 오늘 버스 정기권을 살 수 있을까요?
> B: 어떤 버스 정기권을 사고 싶으세요?
> A: 옵션을 알려주시겠어요?
> B: 하루, 월, 주 단위의 정기권이 있고, 학생 정기권도 있습니다.
> A: 학생 정기권은 얼마인가요?
> B: 정기권은 무료이지만, 다달이 지불하는 스티커는 12달러입니다.
> A: 그럼 그걸로 할게요.
> B: 네, 학생증 좀 주시겠어요?
> A: 네, 여기 있습니다.

① 무임승차 벌금이 얼마인가요
② 어떤 게 가장 합리적이죠
④ 연장에 무슨 조건이 있나요

어휘
pass 정기권 purchase 사다 monthly 다달이 지불하는
penalty 벌금 a free ride 무임승차
reasonable 합리적인 restriction 조건, 제한

정답 ③

DAY 17

167 밑줄 친 부분에 들어갈 말로 가장 적절한 것은?

 Sophia Rodriguez
Hey, Jessica! Have you heard about David?
10:42

 Jessie Thompson
No, what happened?
10:43

 Sophia Rodriguez
He got food poisoning and had to be hospitalized.
10:44

 Jessie Thompson
Oh no, poor David! _____.
10:45

 Sophia Rodriguez
I was thinking the same thing. Maybe some flowers and a get-well card?
10:46

 Jessie Thompson
That sounds perfect.
10:47

 Sophia Rodriguez
Let's meet at the hospital at 4 PM.
10:48

① Hot weather caused my lunch to go bad
② We should bring him something to cheer him up
③ I had no idea which hospital he was admitted to
④ I've had food poisoning before, just like him

168 밑줄 친 부분에 들어갈 말로 가장 적절한 것은?

A: Do you have any plans for the upcoming long weekend?
B: Not yet, but I'm thinking of going hiking if the weather's nice.
A: That sounds like a fun idea. _____?
B: I'm leaning towards that scenic route we talked about last month.
A: Awesome! Can I come with you? I'll bring my camera. It'll be great to capture the views.

① Have you decided on a trail
② Are you familiar with those hiking routes
③ What is the most important thing in a hiking trip
④ Were there any special events you could engage in

문장 분석 및 해설

167 밑줄 친 부분에 들어갈 말로 가장 적절한 것은?

① 날씨가 더워서 내 점심이 상했어
③ 그가 어느 병원에 입원했는지 몰랐어
④ 딱 그처럼 나도 예전에 식중독에 걸렸었어

어휘 food poisoning 식중독   hospitalize 입원시키다
get-well card 쾌유 기원 카드   go bad 상하다
cheer up ~의 기운을 북돋아주다   admit 입원시키다

정답 ②

168 밑줄 친 부분에 들어갈 말로 가장 적절한 것은?

> A: 다가오는 긴 휴일에 무슨 계획 있어?
> B: 아직 없지만 날씨가 좋다면 등산을 가려고 생각 중이야.
> A: 그거 재미난 생각이네. 코스는 결정했어?
> B: 지난달에 우리가 얘기했었던 그 경치 좋은 코스로 마음이 기울고 있어.
> A: 멋진데! 나도 같이 가도 될까? 내 카메라를 가져갈게. 풍경을 포착하면 좋을 거야.

② 그 등산 코스에 익숙하니
③ 등산에서 가장 중요한 점이 무엇이니
④ 네가 참여할만한 어떤 특별한 이벤트라도 있었어

어휘 go hiking 등산을 가다   scenic 경치가 좋은   route 경로
lean (관심이) 기울이다   capture (정확히) 포착하다
trail 코스   engage in ~에 참여하다

정답 ①

DAY 17   143

169 밑줄 친 부분에 들어갈 말로 가장 적절한 것은?

Sarah Johnson
Hello, I'm interested in booking a room at your hotel for a weekend getaway.
10:42

Aloa Hotel
Hi, Sarah! We'd be delighted to assist you. How many nights will you be staying?
10:43

Sarah Johnson
We plan to stay for two nights, from Friday to Sunday.
10:44

Aloa Hotel
Great! Would you like to book a standard room?
10:45

Sarah Johnson
_____.
10:46

Aloa Hotel
We have several suites available for those dates. They offer more space and luxury, though a little bit expensive.
10:47

Sarah Johnson
That would be wonderful. I'll take one of those.
10:48

① Yes, it's ideal for our visit's purpose
② We're looking for something cheaper
③ No, we're interested in an upgrade
④ I'm satisfied with a range of amenities

170 밑줄 친 부분에 들어갈 말로 가장 적절한 것은?

A rapid antigen test for COVID-19 indicates the _____ of the virus only about 90% of the time when the virus actually exists while the result can be positive around 2% of the time when the virus is not in the body.

① absence
② variation
③ presence
④ deprivation

169 밑줄 친 부분에 들어갈 말로 가장 적절한 것은?

Sarah Johnson
안녕하세요, 주말 휴가를 위해 호텔의 방을 예약하고 싶은데요.
10:42

Aloa Hotel
안녕하세요, Sarah! 모시게 되어 기쁩니다. 며칠 동안 묵으실 건가요?
10:43

Sarah Johnson
금요일부터 일요일까지 이틀 밤을 머물 계획이에요.
10:44

Aloa Hotel
좋습니다! 일반실을 예약하시겠어요?
10:45

Sarah Johnson
아니오, 상급 객실에 관심이 있어요.
10:46

Aloa Hotel
그 날짜에 스위트룸이 몇 개가 있습니다. 스위트룸은 조금 비싸기는 하지만 더 넓은 공간과 호화로움을 제공해드립니다.
10:47

Sarah Johnson
그럼 너무 좋을 것 같아요. 그중의 하나로 할게요.
10:48

① 네, 그 방이 우리 방문 목적에 잘 맞아요
② 우리는 더 저렴한 것을 찾고 있어요
④ 다양한 설비에 만족하고 있어요

어휘 book 예약하다 getaway 휴가 available 이용 가능한 luxury 호화로움 expensive 비싼 purpose 목적 amenitis 설비

정답 ③

170

해석 코로나19의 신속 항원 검사는 바이러스가 실제로 존재하는 겨우 90퍼센트 정도의 경우에 바이러스의 존재를 나타내지만, 바이러스가 몸 안에 존재하지 않는 2퍼센트 정도의 경우에도 검사 결과는 양성으로 나올 수 있다.

어휘 rapid antigen test 신속 항원 검사 indicate 나타내다 actually 실제로 exist 존재하다 positive 양성의 absence 부재 variation 변화 presence 존재 deprivation 박탈

근거

A rapid antigen test for COVID-19 indicates the presence of the virus only about 90% of the time when the virus actually exists while the result can be positive around 2% of the time when the virus is not in the body.

정답 ③

주요 어휘 정리
present 참석한 ↔ absent 결석한
presence 존재, 참석 ↔ absence 부재, 결석

171 밑줄 친 부분에 들어갈 말로 가장 적절한 것은?

> His conscience troubled him until he decided to _____ his guilt to the authorities.

① confess   ② conceal
③ embrace   ④ tackle

172 밑줄 친 부분에 들어갈 말로 가장 적절한 것은?

> She showed _____ care in handling delicate flowers in the garden.

① general   ② indifferent
③ tender   ④ tough

173 밑줄 친 부분에 들어갈 말로 가장 적절한 것은?

> A: Hey Mark, did you get a chance to review the sales report?
> B: I did. The numbers are solid, but I think we should push for more in Q4.
> A: Agreed. Should we revise the targets?
> B: I think so. How about increasing them by 10%?
> A: _____
> B: Right. I'll hold the meeting to discuss it with the team members.
> A: Sounds good. Please let me know when you fix the meeting time.

① Wait, we need a debate on it.
② Didn't you go over those figures?
③ Wow, you are definitely decisive.
④ Can you persuade the customers?

171

해석 그의 양심은 그가 당국에 죄를 자백할 때까지 그를 괴롭혔다.

어휘 conscience 양심 trouble 괴롭히다 guilt 죄
authority (pl.) 당국 confess 자백하다 conceal 숨기다
embrace 받아들이다 tackle (문제, 일 등과) 씨름하다

근거

> His conscience troubled him until he decided to confess his guilt to the authorities.

정답 ①

주요 어휘 정리

conceal 숨기다
= hide
  veil

172

해석 그녀는 정원의 섬세한 꽃들을 다루는데 부드러운 손질을 보여주었다.

어휘 care 손질 handle 다루다 delicate 섬세한 general 일반적인
indifferent 무관심한 tender 부드러운 tough 거친

근거

> She showed tender care in handling delicate flowers in the garden.

정답 ③

173 밑줄 친 부분에 들어갈 말로 가장 적절한 것은?

> A: Mark 씨, 판매 보고서를 검토할 기회가 있었나요?
> B: 그랬어요. 수치는 확실하지만 4분기에는 더 많은 것을 추진해야 한다고 생각합니다.
> A: 동의해요. 목표를 수정해야 할까요?
> B: 저도 그렇게 생각해요. 10퍼센트를 늘리는 게 어때요?
> A: 잠시만요, 그 점에 대해 논의가 필요해요.
> B: 그래요. 팀원들과 상의할 수 있도록 회의를 할게요.
> A: 좋아요. 회의 시간이 정해지면 저에게도 알려주세요.

② 그 수치들을 검토하지 않았나요?
③ 와, 확실히 결단력이 있으시네요.
④ 고객들을 설득해주시겠어요?

어휘 review 검토하다 solid 확실한 Q4 사분기 revise 수정하다
target 목표 increase 늘이다 discuss 상의하다 debate 논의
go over ~을 검토하다 figure 수치 definitely 확실히
decisive 결단력이 있는 persuade 설득하다

정답 ①

174 밑줄 친 부분에 들어갈 말로 가장 적절한 것은?

> A: Hi, Maureen. It's great to see you again.
> B: Hi! It's good to see you, too.
> A: I heard you've recently got promoted as a project manager. Congrats.
> B: Thank you! I'm trying my best to fit in.
> A: I envy you. _____.
> B: Don't be depressed. One of these days, your day will come.
> A: You're right. I'll turn over a new leaf.
> B: That's what I'm talking about!

① I'm sure it can be a challenging position
② I'll be able to fit you in this afternoon
③ I kept being passed over for a promotion
④ There is nothing depressing about that

175 밑줄 친 부분에 들어갈 말로 가장 적절한 것은?

> Since dressing rooms were side by side, they decided to _____ the wall so they'd have one large room to themselves.

① build　　②　demolish
③ seize　　④　suppress

176 밑줄 친 부분에 들어갈 말로 가장 적절한 것은?

> The ministries of agriculture and industries have reached an agreement to _____ chicken exports to boost supply in the domestic market and help keep prices in check.

① uphold　　②　purchase
③ ban　　　④　endanger

174 밑줄 친 부분에 들어갈 말로 가장 적절한 것은?

> A: 안녕, Maureen. 다시 만나서 반가워.
> B: 안녕! 나도 만나서 반가워.
> A: 최근에 프로젝트 매니저로 승진했다고 들었어. 축하해.
> B: 고마워! 적응하려고 최선을 다하고 있어.
> A: 부럽다. 나는 계속 승진에서 제외되었는데.
> B: 의기소침해하지 마. 언젠가, 좋은 때가 올 거야.
> A: 맞아. 심기일전하겠어.
> B: 내 말이 그 말이야!

① 분명 힘든 자리가 될 수도 있어
② 오늘 오후에 시간 내서 너를 만날 수 있어
④ 거기엔 전혀 우울한 게 없어

어휘 promote 승진시키다 fit in 적응하다, 시간을 내어~을 만나다
I envy you. 부러워. depressed 의기소침한
one of these days 언젠가
Your day will come. 좋은 때가 올 거야.
turn over a new leaf 심기일전하다
pass over (승진에서) 제외시키다 depressing 우울한

정답 ③

175

해석 탈의실이 나란히 있었기 때문에, 그들은 하나의 큰 방을 독차지하도록 벽을 허물기로 결정했다.

어휘 side by side 나란히 있는 have ~ to oneself ~을 독차지하다
build 세우다 demolish 허물다 seize 압수하다
suppress 진압하다

근거
> Since dressing rooms were side by side, they decided to demolish the wall so they'd have one large room to themselves.

정답 ②

주요 어휘 정리

demolish ~을 허물다	suppress 진압하다
= pull down	= repress
tear down	control
	quell
	put down
	keep down

176

해석 농림부와 산업부는 국내시장에서의 공급을 늘리고 가격을 억제하는 것을 돕기 위해 닭의 수출을 금지하는 합의에 도달했다.

어휘 ministry (정부의) 부 reach an agreement 합의에 도달하다
boost 늘리다 domestic 국내의 keep ~ in check ~을 억제하다
uphold 지지하다 purchase 구입하다
ban 금지하다 endanger 위태롭게 하다

근거
> The ministries of agriculture and industries have reached an agreement to ban chicken exports to boost supply in the domestic market and help keep prices in check.

정답 ③

주요 어휘 정리

uphold 지지하다	ban 금지하다
= support	= prohibit
espouse	exclude
buttress	forbid
prop up	restrain
hold up	inhibit
	proscribe
	block
	bar

177 밑줄 친 부분에 들어갈 말로 가장 적절한 것은?

> A: Hello, Dr. Evans. It's nice to finally meet you.
> B: Pleasure to see you, too.
> A: Can I have your autograph on this?
> B: Oh, it's my new book on quantum mechanics.
> A: Yes, I bought it as soon as it was published.
> B: I guess it could be too hard for lay readers to understand.
> A: _____.
> B: Oh, really? In that case, we can have an in-depth discussion on it.

① I don't know that much about the area
② I'm in the doctoral program in physics
③ You don't need to be that judgmental
④ You can have my book if you want

178 밑줄 친 부분에 들어갈 말로 가장 적절한 것은?

> A: I thought you said you were going to call me last night.
> B: I did, but I got caught up with work and lost track of time.
> A: No worries, I was just wondering what happened.
> B: Actually, there was a reason for it. _____ _____.
> A: Wow, congratulations! How about we celebrate this weekend?
> B: Definitely! Let's make plans.

① I didn't think it was important to you
② I was hoping you would call me first
③ I thought it'd be fun to have it be a surprise
④ I got a promotion, which made me so busy

177 밑줄 친 부분에 들어갈 말로 가장 적절한 것은?

> A: 안녕하세요, Evans 박사님. 마침내 만나게 되어 반갑습니다.
> B: 저도 만나서 기쁘군요.
> A: 여기에 사인을 받을 수 있을까요?
> B: 오, 양자 역학에 관한 제 신간이군요.
> A: 네, 출간되자마자 구매했어요.
> B: 전문 지식이 없는 독자들이 이해하기에는 너무 어려울 것 같은데요.
> A: 저는 물리학 박사과정 프로그램에 재학 중이에요.
> B: 오, 그래요? 그런 경우라면, 우리는 그것에 관해 깊이 있는 토론을 할 수 있겠네요.

① 저는 그 분야에 관해 그렇게 많이 아는 건 아니에요
③ 그렇게 비판적으로 구실 필요는 없잖아요
④ 원하시면 제 책을 가지셔도 됩니다

어휘 autograph 사인   quantum mechanics 양자 역학
lay 전문 지식이 없는   in-depth 깊이 있는   area 분야
doctoral 박사과정의   physics 물리학   judgmental 비판적인

정답 ②

178 밑줄 친 부분에 들어갈 말로 가장 적절한 것은?

> A: 어젯밤에 네가 나에게 전화한다고 말했던 것 같은데.
> B: 그랬지, 그런데 일에 빠져서 시간 가는 줄 몰랐어.
> A: 괜찮아, 단지 무슨 일 생겼는지 걱정했을 뿐이야.
> B: 실은, 그럴 만한 이유가 있었어. 나 승진했어, 그래서 너무 바빴어.
> A: 와우, 축하해! 이번 주말에 우리 축하하는 것이 어떨까?
> B: 물론이지! 계획을 짜자.

① 그것이 너에게 중요하다고 생각하지 않았어
② 네가 나에게 먼저 전화할 거라 기대하고 있었어
③ 깜짝 놀라게 하면 재미있을 것 같았어

어휘 get caught up with ~에 빠져 있다
lose track of time 시간 가는 줄 모르다   No worries. 괜찮아.
promotion 승진   fantastic 엄청난   celebrate 축하하다

정답 ④

179 밑줄 친 부분에 들어갈 말로 가장 적절한 것은?

Sarah Jones: Hi, I have some issues with our recent shipments. 10:42

Tom Kim: Sorry to hear that. What's the problem? 10:43

Sarah Jones: Many items arrived damaged and below our usual standards, which is affecting customer satisfaction. 10:44

Tom Kim: That's definitely concerning. _____? 10:45

Sarah Jones: Sure, I can send you photos and the box numbers of the affected shipments. 10:46

Tom Kim: Thanks. I'll investigate and get back to you with a solution. 10:47

Sarah Jones: Appreciate it. 10:48

① Can you send us a formal complaint paper right now
② Could you please visit us to discuss it further
③ Can you send me specific data to judge the situation
④ Can you take a picture of customers on the ship

180 밑줄 친 부분에 들어갈 말로 가장 적절한 것은?

The tears began to fall faster as Paul couldn't _____ his emotions.

① postpone   ② withhold
③ cause   ④ hinder

179 밑줄 친 부분에 들어갈 말로 가장 적절한 것은?

① 지금 바로 정식 불만 서류를 보내주실 수 있나요
② 그것을 더 논의하기 위해 저희를 방문해 주시겠습니까
④ 배에 타고 있는 고객들의 사진을 찍어주시겠어요

어휘 shipment 배송물 item 품목 satisfaction 만족
investigate 조사하다 get back to ~에게 다시 연락하다
solution 해결책 specific 구체적인

정답 ③

180

해석 Paul이 감정을 억제하지 못하자 눈물이 더 빨리 떨어지기 시작했다.

어휘 tears 눈물 emotion 감정 postpone 미루다
withhold 억제하다 cause 일으키다 hinder 방해하다

근거
The tears began to fall faster as Paul couldn't withhold his emotions.

정답 ②

주요 어휘 정리

postpone 미루다	withhold 억제하다
= delay	= control
suspend	check
defer	hold back
put off	
hold off	hinder 방해하다
	= impede
cause 일으키다	deter
= generate	thwart
produce	hamper
create	disturb
bring about	interrupt
give rise to	set back
touch off	

DAY 18　153

181 밑줄 친 부분에 들어갈 말로 가장 적절한 것은?

> The path to the summit is _____, requiring climbers to use ropes and harnesses.

① sheer   ② plain
③ expensive   ④ steep

182 밑줄 친 부분에 들어갈 말로 가장 적절한 것은?

> While public sector unions have _____ because the public sector itself has grown, private sector unions have been wiped out by globalization.

① withdrawn   ② thrived
③ monopolized   ④ vanished

183 밑줄 친 부분에 들어갈 말로 가장 적절한 것은?

> A: Hi, I'd like to withdraw $1,000 from my account, please.
> B: I'm sorry, but withdrawing $1,000 would bring your balance below the minimum balance.
> A: What happens if I lower the minimum required?
> B: Lowering the minimum balance adversely affects your account's benefits and results in charges.
> A: Hmm, I didn't realize that. In that case, _____.
> B: That's a good idea. Then how much would you like to withdraw?
> A: Just half of what I requested.

① What you've told me makes me want more money
② I want to hold off on withdrawal just in case
③ I would like to increase the minimum balance required
④ I had better close my account for a while

181

해석 산꼭대기로 가는 길은 가팔라서, 등반가들이 로프와 장비의 사용이 필요하다.

어휘 summit 산꼭대기 climber 등반가 harness 장비 sheer 순진한 plain 쉬운 expensive 비싼 steep 가파른

근거

> The path to the summit is steep, requiring climbers to use ropes and harnesses.

정답 ④

주요 어휘 정리

sheer 순전한
= total
  absolute
  utter

plain 쉬운, 평이한
= simple
  easy

182

해석 공공부문의 노조는 공공부문 자체가 성장했기 때문에 번창한 반면에, 민간부문 노조는 세계화로 인해 전멸했다.

어휘 sector 부문 union 노조 wipe out 전멸시키다 withdraw 철회하다 thrive 번창하다 monopolize 독점하다 vanish 사라지다

근거

> While public sector unions have thrived because the public sector itself has grown, private sector unions have been wiped out by globalization.

정답 ②

주요 어휘 정리

withdraw 철회하다
= abolish   revoke
  annul   rescind
  retract   recall
  repeal

thrive 번영하다
= flourish
  prosper
  bloom

vanish 사라지다
= disappear   fade away
  perish   pass away
  die

183 밑줄 친 부분에 들어갈 말로 가장 적절한 것은?

> A: 안녕하세요, 제 계좌에서 1,000달러를 인출하고 싶습니다.
> B: 죄송하지만, 1,000달러를 인출하시면 잔액이 필수 최저한도 밑으로 내려갑니다.
> A: 제가 최소 잔액을 낮추면 어떻게 되나요?
> B: 최소 잔액을 낮추면 고객님의 계좌 혜택에 악영향을 주고 결과적으로 요금도 발생합니다.
> A: 음, 그건 몰랐어요. 그렇다면, 최소 잔액을 올리고 싶어요.
> B: 좋은 생각이십니다. 그러면 얼마를 인출하시겠어요?
> A: 요청한 액수의 절반만요.

① 당신 말을 듣고 보니 더 많은 돈을 원하게 되네요
② 만약을 위해서 인출을 보류하고 싶어요
④ 제 계좌를 당분간 닫아버리는 게 낫겠어요

어휘 withdraw 인출하다 account 계좌 balance 잔액 minimum 최소의 adversely affect 악영향을 주다 benefit 혜택 charge 요금 hold off on ~을 보류하다 just in case 만약을 위해서 for a while 당분간

정답 ③

DAY 19   155

184 밑줄 친 부분에 들어갈 말로 가장 적절한 것은?

> There are two very different kinds of people; some spend money as often as possible on something as _____ as fancy goods and pens, while others spend money less frequently but on expensive luxury goods such as cars and watches.

① indolent ② momentous
③ arid ④ frivolous

185 밑줄 친 부분에 들어갈 말로 가장 적절한 것은?

> In the Third World, many pirate publishers _____ copyrights by illegally copying copyrighted books from developed countries.

① infringe ② salvage
③ rebel ④ capture

186 밑줄 친 부분에 들어갈 말로 가장 적절한 것은?

> A: Where would you like me to take you?
> B: I need to go to Gangnam Station.
> A: That's no problem. Please fasten your seat belt.
> B: How long is the ride?
> A: It'll be about 25 minutes.
> B: _____?
> A: That's as quick as I can do it.

① Can you get me there faster
② Is there any station near here
③ Is there any other way to get there
④ Can you take over the wheel

184

해석 매우 다른 두 종류의 사람들이 있다; 어떤 사람들은 팬시 상품과 펜 같은 사소한 것에 가능한 한 자주 돈을 쓰는 반면, 어떤 사람들은 돈을 덜 자주 쓰지만 자동차와 시계와 같은 값비싼 사치품에 쓴다.

어휘 fancy goods (선물용, 장식용) 팬시 상품   frequently 자주
luxury goods 사치품   indolent 게으른   momentous 중요한
arid 매우 건조한   frivolous 사소한

근거

> There are two very different kinds of people; some spend money as often as possible on something as frivolous as fancy goods and pens, while others spend money less frequently but on expensive luxury goods such as cars and watches.

정답 ④

주요 어휘 정리

frivolous 사소한
= trivial   insignificant
  trifling   negligible
  petty   banal
  minor   trite
  unimportant   niggling

185

해석 제 3세계에서는 많은 해적 출판사들이 선진국의 저작권이 있는 책들을 불법 복제함으로써 저작권을 침해한다.

어휘 pirate 해적의   publisher 출판사   developed country 선진국
infringe 침해하다   salvage 구조하다   rebel 반항하다
capture 사로잡다

근거

> In the Third World, many pirate publishers infringe copyrights by illegally copying copyrighted books from developed countries.

정답 ①

주요 어휘 정리

infringe 침해하다   salvage 구조하다
= encroach   = save
  trespass   rescue

rebel 반항하다   capture 사로잡다
= oppose   = captivate
  resist   fascinate
  disobey   enchant
  defy

186 밑줄 친 부분에 들어갈 말로 가장 적절한 것은?

> A: 어디로 모셔다드릴까요?
> B: 강남역으로 가주세요.
> A: 문제 없습니다. 안전띠를 매주세요.
> B: 얼마나 걸리나요?
> A: 약 25분 걸립니다.
> B: 더 빨리 갈 수 있을까요?
> A: 이게 제가 할 수 있는 한 최대한 빨리 가는 겁니다.

② 여기 근처에 역이 있나요
③ 거기까지 가는 다른 길이 있나요
④ 대신 운전해줄 수 있나요

어휘 fasten one's seat belt 안전 벨트를 매다
take over the wheel 대신 운전하다

정답 ①

DAY 19

187 밑줄 친 부분에 들어갈 말로 가장 적절한 것은?

Liz Mongomery: My house was robbed last night. 10:42

Theo Lincoln: Are you serious? Did you report to the police? 10:43

Liz Mongomery: I did, and it is under investigation. 10:44

Theo Lincoln: How did that happen? 10:45

Liz Mongomery: I think _____. 10:47

Theo Lincoln: You should have taken security seriously. 10:48

Liz Mongomery: You're right. I should be more careful from now on. 10:49

① the robber busted my window
② I know who did this
③ he set the door alarm
④ I forgot to lock the door

188 밑줄 친 부분에 들어갈 말로 가장 적절한 것은?

A: I need to finalize the budget report by the end of the day. Can you check if all the figures are accurate?

B: Sure, I'll review the numbers and let you know if there are any discrepancies.

A: That would be very nice. _____

B: Oh, I should get it done by 3 PM because I'll have to prepare the project proposal.

① I think I am good at numbers and math.
② There are many discrepancies between us.
③ Will you send me the revised version?
④ When do you expect to finish the work?

문장 분석 및 해설

187 밑줄 친 부분에 들어갈 말로 가장 적절한 것은?

① 강도가 창문을 부순 것
② 누가 했는지 아는 것
③ 그가 현관 경보 장치를 설치한 것

어휘 rob 강도질을 하다 investigation 수사 security 보안
bust 부수다 door alarm 현관 경보 장치

정답 ④

188 밑줄 친 부분에 들어갈 말로 가장 적절한 것은?

> A: 오늘까지 예산 보고를 마무리해야 하는데, 혹시 수치가 모두 정확한지 확인해 주실 수 있나요?
> B: 물론이죠, 숫자를 검토하고 일치하지 않는 것이 있으면 알려드리겠습니다.
> A: 그러면 아주 좋겠네요. 그 일을 언제 끝낼 것으로 예상하세요?
> B: 오, 프로젝트 기획안을 준비해야 해서 오후 3시까지는 끝내야만 해요.

① 저는 숫자와 수학을 잘하는 것 같아요.
② 우리 사이에는 많은 차이점이 있어요.
③ 수정된 버전을 제게 보내주시겠어요?

어휘 finalize 마무리하다 budget 예산 figure 수치 accurate 정확한
discrepancy 불일치, 차이점 proposal 기획안 revised 수정된

정답 ④

189 밑줄 친 부분에 들어갈 말로 가장 적절한 것은?

Sophie: Have you tried that new Italian restaurant in town? 10:42

Matt: Not yet, but I've heard that it's good. Have you? 10:43

Sophie: Yeah, I went there yesterday. The pasta was amazing! 10:44

Matt: _____. 10:45

Sophie: I'm down! How about Friday night? 10:46

Matt: Friday works. Let's say 7 PM? 10:47

Sophie: Perfect. I'll make a reservation. 10:48

Matt: Great! Looking forward to it. 10:49

① The Italian pasta is my comfort food
② Reservation is needed in that case
③ We should go together sometime, then
④ The store is always full on Fridays

190 밑줄 친 부분에 들어갈 말로 가장 적절한 것은?

The hotel offered _____ breakfast for guests staying in their deluxe suites, allowing them to start their day with a delicious meal at no extra cost.

① spontaneous   ② artificial
③ complimentary ④ excessive

189 밑줄 친 부분에 들어갈 말로 가장 적절한 것은?

① 이탈리아식 파스타는 나를 편하게 하는 음식이에요
② 그런 경우라면 예약이 필요해요
④ 그 가게는 금요일이면 항상 가득 차요

어휘 I'm down! 나도 좋아! comfort food 편하게 하는 음식

정답 ③

190

해석 호텔은 디럭스 스위트룸에 투숙하는 투숙객들을 위해 무료 조식을 제공해 추가 비용 없이 맛있는 식사로 하루를 시작할 수 있도록 했다.

어휘 guest 투숙객 deluxe suite 디럭스 스위트룸 extra 추가의 cost 비용 spontaneous 즉흥적인 artificial 인위적인 complimentary 무료의 excessive 과도한

근거

> The hotel offered complimentary breakfast for guests staying in their deluxe suites, allowing them to start their day with a delicious meal at no extra cost.

정답 ③

주요 어휘 정리

complimentary 무료의
= free
  included
  provided

spontaneous 즉흥적인
= impromtu
  unplanned
  unrehearsed
  improvised
  ad-lib

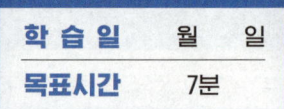

191 밑줄 친 부분에 들어갈 말로 가장 적절한 것은?

> Despite facing challenges, their friendship remained _____ over the years.

① timid ② tentative
③ capricious ④ constant

192 밑줄 친 부분에 들어갈 말로 가장 적절한 것은?

> Acute illnesses are usually quick and treatable, but _____ illnesses are long-term and usually require treatment for the rest of your life.

① chronic ② adverse
③ recessive ④ nocturnal

193 밑줄 친 부분에 들어갈 말로 가장 적절한 것은?

> A: Hello, can I get a copy of my resident registration?
> B: Hi, no problem! Do you have your resident ID card with you?
> A: Oh, my gosh! I must have left it at home.
> B: Do you have _____?
> A: Let me see. Thanks god! I've brought my driver's license.
> B: That works. Just wait for a second or two. It won't take long.

① your driver's license with you when driving a car
② anything with your photo issued by the government
③ knowledge or experience in dealing with this situation
④ time to read the guidelines before requesting documents

191

해석 어려움에 직면했지만, 그들의 우정은 수년간 계속 변함없었다.

어휘 face 직면하다   challenge 어려움   timid 소심한
tentative 잠정적인   capricious 변덕스러운   constant 변함없는

근거

> Despite facing challenges, their friendship remained constant over the years.

정답 ④

주요 어휘 정리

constant 변함없는	capricious 변덕스러운
= incessant	= changeable
ceaseless	mutable
permanent	variable
perpetual	fluctuant
perennial	

192

해석 급성 질환은 보통 순식간이고 치료할 수 있지만, 만성 질환은 장기적이고 보통 남은 평생 동안 치료를 필요로 한다.

어휘 acute 급성의   treatable 치료할 수 있는   treatment 치료
chronic 만성의   adverse 불리한   recessive 열성의
nocturnal 야행성의

근거

> Acute illnesses are usually quick and treatable, but chronic illnesses are long-term and usually require treatment for the rest of your life.

정답 ①

주요 어휘 정리

chronic 만성적인	↔	acute 급성의
adverse 불리한	↔	beneficial 유리한
recessive 열성의	↔	dominant 우성의
nocturnal 야행성의	↔	diurnal 주행성의

193 밑줄 친 부분에 들어갈 말로 가장 적절한 것은?

> A: 안녕하세요, 주민등록등본을 뗄 수 있을까요?
> B: 안녕하세요, 물론이죠! 주민등록증을 가지고 오셨나요?
> A: 오, 맙소사! 집에 두고 왔나 봐요.
> B: 정부에서 발행한 사진이 붙은 어떤 것이든 가지고 있나요?
> A: 잠시만요. 다행이다! 제 운전면허증을 가지고 왔네요.
> B: 그거면 됩니다. 아주 잠시만 기다려주세요. 오래 걸리지 않을 거예요.

① 차를 운전할 때 운전면허증을
③ 이런 상황을 다루는 지식이나 경험을
④ 서류를 요청하기 전에 지침을 읽어볼 시간을

어휘 copy of resident registration 주민등록등본
resident ID card 주민등록증   issue 발행하다
deal with ~을 다루다   guideline 지침   request 요청하다

정답 ②

194 밑줄 친 부분에 들어갈 말로 가장 적절한 것은?

> A: I need to book a hotel for my trip next month.
> B: Sure! Do you have a specific location in mind?
> A: Yes, I'd like to stay near the city center.
> B: _____
> A: Four nights, from the 10th to the 14th.
> B: Okay, would you prefer a standard room or a suite?
> A: A standard room is fine. Can you check for available options?
> B: Of course! I'll find the best rates and let you know.

① Do you have a preferred check-in time?
② Do you want a city view or a garden view?
③ How many nights will you be staying?
④ How many people will be staying in the room?

195 밑줄 친 부분에 들어갈 말로 가장 적절한 것은?

> The new restaurant in town offers a diverse menu of delicious dishes at _____ prices, making it a favorite among budget-conscious diners.

① irrational   ② affordable
③ superior   ④ prosperous

196 밑줄 친 부분에 들어갈 말로 가장 적절한 것은?

> It is speculated that if the recent economic recession continues unabated, the number of unemployed people will _____ to uncontrollable levels, which in turn, will lead to more serious economic breakdown.

① dwindle   ② soar
③ persist   ④ ameliorate

194 밑줄 친 부분에 들어갈 말로 가장 적절한 것은?

> A: 다음 달 여행을 위해 호텔을 예약해야 해요.
> B: 네! 생각하고 계신 특정 위치가 있으신가요?
> A: 네, 도심부 근처에 머물고 싶어요.
> B: 몇 박을 머무실 건가요?
> A: 4박이요, 10일부터 14일까지요.
> B: 알겠습니다. 일반 객실을 원하시나요, 아니면 스위트룸을 원하시나요?
> A: 일반 객실이면 돼요. 가능한 옵션을 확인해 줄 수 있나요?
> B: 물론이죠! 최적의 가격을 찾아서 알려드릴게요.

① 선호하는 체크인 시간이 있나요?
② 도시 전망을 원하시나요, 정원 전망을 원하시나요?
④ 방에 몇 명이 묵을 예정인가요?

어휘 book 예약하다 have ~ in mind ~을 생각하다 specific 특정한 location 위치 city center 도심부 standard 일반적인 suite 스위트룸 rate 가격

정답 ③

195

해석 마을의 새로운 식당은 다양한 메뉴의 맛있는 요리를 저렴한 가격에 제공하여, 가격을 중시하는 손님들 사이에 가장 인기 있는 곳이 되었다.

어휘 diverse 다양한 dish 요리 favorite 가장 인기 있는 것[곳] budget-conscious 가격을 중시하는 diner (식당의) 손님 irrational 비이성적인 affordable 저렴한 superior 우월한 prosperous 번성하는

근거
> The new restaurant in town offers a diverse menu of delicious dishes at affordable prices, making it a favorite among budget-conscious diners.

정답 ②

주요 어휘 정리
affordable 저렴한
= reasonable
  low
  competitive
  budget-friendly
  economical

196

해석 만일 최근의 경제 불황이 수그러들지 않고 지속되면, 실업자의 수는 통제할 수 없는 수준까지 치솟을 것이고, 이는 결국 더 심각한 경제 붕괴를 초래할 것이라고 예상된다.

어휘 speculate 예상하다 recession 불황 unabated 수그러들지 않는 uncontrollable 통제할 수 없는 in turn 결국 breakdown 붕괴 dwindle 줄어들다 soar 치솟다 persist 지속하다 ameliorate 개선되다

근거
> It is speculated that if the recent economic recession continues unabated, the number of unemployed people will soar to uncontrollable levels, which in turn, will lead to more serious economic breakdown.

정답 ②

주요 어휘 정리

dwindle 줄어들다	soar 치솟다
= reduce	= rise
decline	surge
decrease	skyrocket
diminish	proliferate

197 밑줄 친 부분에 들어갈 말로 가장 적절한 것은?

> A: How's my dog doing? Any updates?
> B: He's stable but still under observation for a respiratory infection.
> A: I hope he gets better soon. _____?
> B: Just visit him and keep him calm. We'll update you if anything changes.
> A: Got it. Thanks!

① Can I take him home now
② Is there anything I can do
③ Should I drug him regularly
④ Will he be hospitalized

198 밑줄 친 부분에 들어갈 말로 가장 적절한 것은?

Michelle Lee
Hello, I'm having trouble with my recent order. The item arrived damaged.
10:42

Customer Service
Sorry, could you please provide me with your order number and a photo of the damaged item?
10:43

Michelle Lee
Sure, my order number is #12345. I've attached a photo of the item.
10:44

Customer Service
Thank you for the information. We'll review the photo and process a replacement or refund for you.
10:45

Michelle Lee
_____?
10:46

Customer Service
It usually takes 3-5 business days to resolve such issues. We'll update you as soon as possible.
10:47

Michelle Lee
Great, thank you for your help.
10:48

Customer Service
You're welcome! If you have any other questions, feel free to ask.
10:49

① How long will this process take
② Can I exchange it for a different color
③ Do you want me to tell you the refund account
④ Are those sold again as refurbished products

197 밑줄 친 부분에 들어갈 말로 가장 적절한 것은?

> A: 제 강아지는 어떤가요? 새로운 소식이 있나요?
> B: 안정적이지만 여전히 호흡기 감염병을 관찰받고 있는 중이에요.
> A: 강아지가 빨리 나아지면 좋겠어요. 제가 할 수 있는 일이 있을까요?
> B: 그냥 면회 오셔서 진정 상태를 유지시켜 주세요. 변화가 있으면 알려드리겠습니다.
> A: 알겠습니다. 고맙습니다.

① 지금 집으로 데려갈 수 있을까요
③ 제가 약을 규칙적으로 먹여야 하나요
④ 입원시켜야 할까요

어휘 update 새로운 소식; (최신 정보를) 알려주다   stable 안정적인   under observation 관찰받는   respiratory 호흡기의   infection 감염(병)   get better (병이) 나아지다   drug 약을 먹이다   regularly 규칙적으로   hospitalize 입원시키다

정답 ②

198 밑줄 친 부분에 들어갈 말로 가장 적절한 것은?

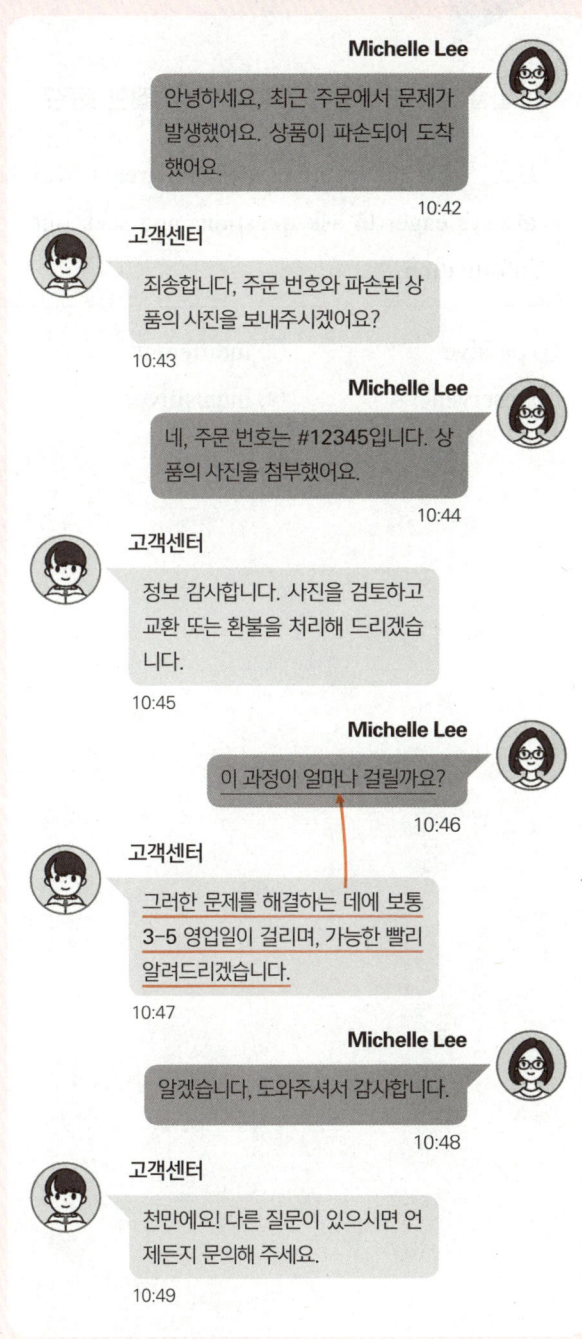

② 다른 색으로 바꿀 수 있을까요
③ 환불 계좌를 알려드릴까요
④ 그런 것들은 리퍼브 상품으로 다시 팔리나요

어휘 recent 최근의   damaged 파손된   attach 첨부하다   replacement 교환   refund 환불   exchange 교환하다   account 계좌   refurbished product 리퍼브 상품: 결함이 있었던 제품을 수리해 다시 판매하는 제품

정답 ①

199 밑줄 친 부분에 들어갈 말로 가장 적절한 것은?

> Her _____ nature made her a great researcher, always eager to ask questions and seek out new information.

① passive   ② indifferent
③ reserved ④ inquisitive

200 밑줄 친 부분에 들어갈 말로 가장 적절한 것은?

> A: Excuse me, can you help me with directions to the conference center?
> B: Sure! Head straight down this street for two blocks, then take a right.
> A: Okay, two blocks and then right. After that?
> B: You'll see a big park on your left. The conference center is just past it.
> A: Got it. _____?
> B: Uhh, it's ten times the size of a soccer field.
> A: What? It's not within walking distance.
> B: Sounds about right.

① Have you visited the conference center before
② How long do you think it will take to get there
③ Just for calculating travel time, how big is the park
④ Do you like playing soccer more than basketball

199

해석 그녀의 호기심 많은 성격은 그녀를 훌륭한 연구자로 만들었고, 항상 질문을 하고 새로운 정보를 찾기에 열심이었다.

어휘 nature 성격   eager 열심인   seek out 찾다   passive 수동적인
indifferent 무관심한   reserved 내성적인
inquisitive 호기심 많은

근거

> Her inquisitive nature made her a great researcher, always eager to ask questions and seek out new information.

정답 ④

주요 어휘 정리

reserved 내성적인, 말이 없는 ↔ outgoing 외향적인
= reticent
  quiet
  private

inquisitive 호기심 많은
= curious

200 밑줄 친 부분에 들어갈 말로 가장 적절한 것은?

> A: 실례합니다. 컨퍼런스 센터로 가는 길을 알려주시겠어요?
> B: 물론이죠! 이 길을 따라 두 블록 정도 직진한 후 우회전하세요.
> A: 좋아요, 두 블록을 지나 오른쪽으로요. 그다음은요?
> B: 왼쪽에 큰 공원이 보일 거예요. 컨퍼런스 센터는 그곳을 지나면 있습니다.
> A: 알겠습니다. 그저 이동 시간을 계산하려고 그러는데요, 공원이 얼마나 큰가요?
> B: 어, 축구장의 열 배 크기에요.
> A: 네? 걸을 수 있는 거리는 아니네요.
> B: 아마 그럴 것 같네요.

① 컨퍼런스 센터를 예전에 방문한 적이 있나요
② 그곳에 도착하기까지 시간이 얼마나 걸릴까요
④ 농구보다 축구 하는 것을 더 좋아하시나요

어휘 direction 방향   head 가다
within walking distance 걸을 수 있는 거리   calculate 계산하다
travel time 이동 시간

정답 ③